THE ITIVUTTAKA
The Buddha's Sayings

THE ITIVUTTAKA

The Buddha's Sayings

Translated from the Pali by

John D. Ireland

BUDDHIST PUBLICATION SOCIETY
KANDY SRI LANKA

Published in 1991

Buddhist Publication Society
P.O. Box 61
54, Sangharaja Mawatha
Kandy, Sri Lanka

ISBN 955-24-0066-X

Typeset at the BPS using an Atari 1040ST
computer and Signum 2.0 software.

Printed in Sri Lanka by
Karunaratne & Sons Ltd.,
647, Kularatne Mawatha
Colombo-10.

CONTENTS

INTRODUCTION

The present work offers a translation of the Itivuttaka, a collection of 112 short discourses of the Buddha in both prose and verse. The text belongs to the Pali Canon of the Theravada school, being placed between the Udāna and the Sutta Nipāta. It was previously translated by F. L. Woodward and published together with his translation of the Udāna in *Minor Anthologies of the Pali Canon*, Vol. II (London, 1935).

According to the commentarial tradition, the suttas or discourses of the Itivuttaka were collected by the woman lay-disciple Khujjuttarā from sermons given by the Buddha while he was staying at Kosambī. Khujjuttarā was a servant of Sāmāvatī, the consort of King Udena. She had become a stream-enterer after meeting the Buddha and subsequently converted the women of the palace headed by Sāmāvatī to the teaching. She used to go regularly to listen to the Buddha and then later repeated what she had heard to the other women. The collection of these sayings became the Itivuttaka. It is said that the emphatic statements at the beginning and end of each of the suttas, reproduced here only in the first and last, were made by Khujjuttarā to stress that they were the Buddha's words and not her own.

Whether or not this story is true, the Itivuttaka is the only book in the Pali Canon that introduces and concludes its suttas in this fashion, and it is from the opening statement that the title is derived: "This was said *(vuttaṁ)* by the Lord . . . so *(iti)* I heard"—hence *Itivuttaka*, "The So-was-said" or "Sayings."

These "Sayings" are grouped into four unequal sections arranged, like the Anguttara Nikāya, according to the number of items they contain, from one to four. Besides these four sections—The Ones, The Twos, The Threes and The Fours—the text is further subdivided into *vaggas*, groups of roughly ten suttas. But to simplify the presentation, in this translation these sub-groupings have been ignored. Only the four main sections have been retained and the suttas numbered from 1 to 112, as in the PTS edition. A number of the suttas and verses are also found in other parts of the Sutta Piṭaka, especially the Anguttara Nikāya, but many are unique to this collection.

In translating the Itivuttaka I attempted to follow the text as closely as possible and to produce an exact and literal rendition. With the verses, however, while remaining faithful to the meaning, I occasionally found it necessary to depart from the syntax of the Pali. Although I did not attempt to produce a metrical translation, by transposing lines and words and controlling the number of syllables in the line, I aimed at producing a readable and rhythmic English rendering of the original Pali verse.

In this translation of the Itivuttaka, as in my rendering of the Udāna (*The Udāna: Inspired Utterances of the Buddha*, BPS 1990), a few words have been left untranslated. *Dhamma* is the "real truth," the "essential idea" and the "ideal" of the Buddha's teaching. When this Dhamma is revealed to others, the person who understands it is able to attain the final aim of the teaching: to overcome suffering and realise Nibbāna, the ultimate goal.

The word *bhikkhu* is often translated as "monk," but at the time of the Buddha it was not used in such a general sense. A bhikkhu can be defined as "one who is dependent upon another's gifts of alms as his means of subsistence" (see Suttas 91 and 107), but "almsman" or "beggar," the literal meaning, would be quite misleading as it does not imply the honoured status accorded to the bhikkhu. The feminine is *bhikkhunī*, a Buddhist nun, mentioned only occasionally in the present work. Ordinary people called the Buddha's followers "recluses" *(samaṇa)*, which approximates more to what we understand as a "monk" or celibate. A *samaṇa* was one who had actually forsaken the confined and circumscribed family life of a householder. But in later times this general term tended to be used less often when the Sangha, the monastic community, had become well established, identifiable and settled. In the earliest period the Buddha usually used the word "bhikkhu" when addressing his following of *samaṇas* and the same word was used by the monks amongst themselves and by the inner circle of faithful lay-followers who were established in the Dhamma. And it is to these that the Itivuttaka and the other suttas of the Pali Canon were originally directed.

Mention is also made in the Itivuttaka of the *devas.* These are gods, inhabitants of the heavenly worlds, but they are also mortal beings subject to fall when the good kamma that brought them to that realm is exhausted (see Sutta 83). Above the devas are the *brahmās*, high divinities still more powerful than the devas but likewise transient. Their chief is Mahā Brahmā, "the Great Brahmā," who sometimes deludedly fancies himself to be an omnipotent creator.

This translation was made from the Pali Text Society edition of the Itivuttaka, but other editions of the text, especially the Burmese Chaṭṭhasangāyana edition, were also consulted for alternative readings of doubtful passages and for clearing up mistakes and omissions in the text, fortunately few in number. This is in marked contrast to the PTS edition of the Udāna, which is full of errors. In compiling the notes frequent use was made of the commentary, the *Paramatthadīpanī* of Ācariya Dhammapāla. To understand a text, in the places where the use of a word or phrase is ambiguous, the commentary is essential for deciding the traditional meaning and significance of these passages.

The titles of the suttas are taken from the Burmese edition of the text. The PTS edition does not include them, though they can be deduced from the summaries found at the end of each *vagga*. Woodward also does not give them in his translation. The use of initial titles is actually a modern innovation of the printed book. The tradition in Pali literature is either the end-name—often several alternatives are given for important works—or else the summary at the end of the *vagga*, making use of one or more key-words from each of the suttas. The summaries originally served as a device to aid memory in an oral tradition which lacked the benefit of the printed word.

JOHN D. IRELAND

THE ITIVUTTAKA

The Buddha's Sayings

Namo tassa bhagavato arahato
sammā-sambuddhassa

1
THE SECTION OF THE ONES

1 Greed

This was said by the Lord, said by the Arahant, so I heard:[1]

"Abandon one thing, bhikkhus, and I guarantee you non-returning. What is that one thing? Greed is that one thing, bhikkhus. Abandon that and I guarantee you non-returning."[2]

This is the meaning of what the Lord said. So in regard to this it was said:[1]

Beings coveting with greed
Go to rebirth in a bad bourn.[3]
But having rightly understood greed,
Those with insight abandon it.
By abandoning it they never come
Back to this world again.

This too is the meaning of what was said by the Lord, so I heard.[1]

2 Hate

This was said by the Lord . . . .

" . . . Hate is that one thing, bhikkhus.[4] Abandon that and I guarantee you non-returning."

Beings corrupted by hate
Go to rebirth in a bad bourn.
But having rightly understood hate,
Those with insight abandon it.
By abandoning it they never come
Back to this world again.

3 Delusion

This was said by the Lord . . . .

" . . . Delusion is that one thing, bhikkhus. Abandon that and I guarantee you non-returning."

Beings confused by delusion
Go to rebirth in a bad bourn.
But having rightly understood delusion,
Those with insight abandon it.
By abandoning it they never come
Back to this world again.

4 Anger

This was said by the Lord . . . .

" . . . Anger is that one thing, bhikkhus. Abandon that and I guarantee you non-returning."

Beings enraged with anger
Go to rebirth in a bad bourn.
But having rightly understood anger,
Those with insight abandon it.
By abandoning it they never come
Back to this world again.

5 Contempt

This was said by the Lord . . . .

" . . . Contempt is that thing, bhikkhus. Abandon that and I guarantee you non-returning."

Beings despising others with contempt
Go to rebirth in a bad bourn.
But having rightly understood contempt,
Those with insight abandon it.
By abandoning it they never come
Back to this world again.

6 Conceit

This was said by the Lord . . . .

" . . . Conceit is that one thing, bhikkhus. Abandon that and I guarantee you non-returning."

Beings puffed up with conceit
Go to rebirth in a bad bourn.
But having rightly understood conceit,
Those with insight abandon it.
By abandoning it they never come
Back to this world again.

7 Understanding the All

This was said by the Lord . . . .

"Bhikkhus, one who has not directly known and fully understood the 'All,'[5] who has not detached his mind from it and abandoned it, is incapable of destroying suffering. But one who has directly known and fully understood the 'All,' and who has detached his mind from it and abandoned it, is capable of destroying suffering."

One who knows the "All" in every way,
Who is not attached to anything,
Having fully understood the "All,"
Has overcome all suffering.

8 Understanding Conceit

This was said by the Lord . . . .

"Bhikkhus, one who has not directly known and fully understood conceit, who has not detached his mind from it and abandoned it, is incapable of destroying suffering. But one who has directly known and fully understood conceit, and who has detached his mind from it and abandoned it, is capable of destroying suffering."

Humankind is possessed by conceit,
Bound by conceit and delighted with being;
Not fully understanding conceit,
They come again to renewal of being.[6]

But those who have abandoned conceit,
And by destroying conceit are freed,
Have conquered the bondage of conceit
And overcome all suffering.

9-13 Understanding Greed, Etc.

This was said by the Lord . . . .

" . . . One who has directly known and fully understood greed, hate, delusion, anger, contempt . . . is capable of destroying suffering."[7]

14 Ignorance

This was said by the Lord . . . .

"Bhikkhus, I do not perceive any single hindrance other than the hindrance of ignorance by which humankind is so obstructed and for so long a time runs on and wanders in saṁsāra.[8] It is indeed through the hindrance of ignorance that humankind is obstructed and for a long time runs on and wanders in saṁsāra."

No other single thing exists
Like the hindrance of delusion,
Which so obstructs humankind
And makes it wander on forever.

Those who have abandoned delusion,
Cleaving through this mass of darkness,
No longer roam and wander on;
In them the cause is found no more.

15 Craving

This was said by the Lord . . . .

"Bhikkhus, I do not perceive any single fetter other than the fetter of craving by which beings are so tied and for so long a time run on and wander in saṁsāra. It is indeed through the fetter of craving that beings are tied and for a long time run on and wander in saṁsāra."

A man companioned by craving
Wanders on this long journey;
He cannot go beyond saṁsāra
In this state of being or another.

Having understood the danger thus —
That craving is the origin of suffering —
A bhikkhu should wander mindfully,
Free from craving, without grasping.

16 The Learner

This was said by the Lord . . . .

"Bhikkhus, in regard to internal factors, I do not perceive another single factor so helpful as wise attention[9] to a bhikkhu who is a learner, who has not attained perfection but lives aspiring for the supreme security from bondage.[10] Bhikkhus, a bhikkhu who wisely attends abandons what is unwholesome and develops what is wholesome."

For a bhikkhu who is a learner
There is no other thing so helpful
For reaching the highest goal
As the factor wise attention.
Wisely striving a bhikkhu may attain
The destruction of all suffering.

17 The Good Friend

This was said by the Lord . . . .

"Bhikkhus, in regard to external factors, I do not perceive another single factor so helpful as good friendship to a bhikkhu who is a learner, who has not attained perfection but lives aspiring for the supreme security from bondage.[11] Bhikkhus, a bhikkhu who has a good friend abandons what is unwholesome and develops what is wholesome."

When a bhikkhu has good friends,
And is reverential and respectful,
Doing what his friends advise,
Clearly comprehending and mindful,
He may progressively attain
The destruction of all fetters.[12]

18 Disunity in the Sangha

This was said by the Lord . . . .

"There is one thing, bhikkhus, which, when it appears in the world, appears to the detriment of many persons, to the misery of many persons, to the loss, detriment and suffering of devas and humans. What is that one thing? It is disunity in the Sangha.[13] When the Sangha is divided there are mutual quarrels, mutual recriminations, mutual denigrations and mutual expulsions. In this situation those who are unsympathetic are not converted and some who are sympathetic change their minds."[14]

One who divides the Sangha
Abides in a state of misery, in hell,
For the aeon's full duration.
Delighting in dissent, unrighteous,
He is deprived of security from bondage;
By dividing a unified Sangha
He suffers in hell for an aeon.[15]

19 Unity in the Sangha

This was said by the Lord . . . .

"There is one thing, bhikkhus, which, when it appears in the world, appears to the benefit of many persons, to the happiness of many persons, to the gain, benefit and happiness of devas and humans. What is that one thing? It is unity in the Sangha. When the Sangha is united there are no mutual quarrels, mutual recriminations, mutual denigrations and mutual expulsions. In this situation those who are unsympathetic are converted and those who are sympathetic increase in faith."

Pleasant is unity in the Sangha.
One who helps those in unity,
Who delights in unity and is righteous,
Is not deprived of security from bondage.[16]
By making the Sangha united
He rejoices in heaven for an aeon.

20 A Corrupt Mind

This was said by the Lord . . . .

"Here, bhikkhus, some person has a corrupt mind. Having examined his mind with my mind, I know that if this person were to die at this time, as if carried there he would be placed in hell.[17] What is the reason for that? It is because his mind is corrupt. It is because of the mind's corruption that some beings here, when the body perishes, are reborn after death in a state of misery, a bad bourn, a state of ruin, hell."

Understanding the corrupt mind
Of some person dwelling here,
The Buddha explained its meaning
In the presence of the bhikkhus.

If that person were to die
At this very moment now,
He would be reborn in hell
Because of his corrupt mind.

As if they were carried off
And placed there, thus
Beings go to a bad bourn
Because of mind's corruption.[18]

21 A Confident Mind

This was said by the Lord . . . .

"Here, bhikkhus, some person has a confident mind.[19] Having examined his mind with my mind, I know that if this person were to die at this time, as if carried there he would be placed in heaven. What is the reason for that? It is because his mind is confident. It is because of the mind's confidence that some beings here, when the body perishes, are reborn after death in a good bourn, in a heavenly world."

Understanding the confident mind
Of some person dwelling here,
The Buddha explained its meaning
In the presence of the bhikkhus.

If that person were to die
At this very moment now,
He would arise in a good bourn
Because of his confident mind.

As if they were carried off
And placed there, thus
Beings go to a good bourn
Because of mind's confidence.

22 Meritorious Deeds

This was said by the Lord . . . .

"Bhikkhus, do not fear meritorious deeds. This is an expression denoting happiness, what is desirable, wished for, dear and agreeable, that is, 'meritorious deeds.' For I know full well,[20] bhikkhus, that for a long time I experienced desirable, wished for, dear and agreeable results from often performing meritorious deeds.

"Having cultivated for seven years a mind of loving-kindness,[21] for seven aeons of contraction and expansion I did not return to this world. Whenever the aeon contracted I reached the plane of Streaming Radiance and when the aeon expanded I arose in an empty Brahma-mansion. And there I was a Brahmā, the Great Brahmā, the Unvanquished Victor, the All-seeing, the All-powerful.[22] Thirty-six times I was Sakka, the ruler of the devas.[23] And many hundreds of times I was a Wheel-turning Monarch, righteous, a king of righteousness, conqueror of the four quarters of the earth, maintaining stability in the land, in possession of the seven jewels.[24] What need is there to speak of mere local kingship?

"It occurred to me, bhikkhus, to wonder: 'Of what kind of deed of mine is this the fruit? Of what deed's ripening is it that I am now of such great accomplishment and power?' And then it occurred to me: 'It is the fruit of three kinds of deeds of mine, the ripening of three kinds of deeds that I am now of such great accomplishment and power: deeds of giving, of self-mastery and of refraining.'"[25]

One should train in deeds of merit
That yield long-lasting happiness:
Generosity, a balanced life,
Developing a loving mind.

By cultivating these three things,
Deeds yielding happiness,
The wise person is reborn in bliss
In an untroubled happy world.

23 Diligence

This was said by the Lord . . . .

"There is one thing, bhikkhus, developed and continually practised, by which both kinds of welfare are acquired and maintained: welfare here and now, and that pertaining to the future. What is that one thing? It is diligence in wholesome things.[26] This is that one thing, bhikkhus . . . ."

The wise praise diligence
In doing deeds of merit;
For one who is wise and diligent
Obtains a twofold benefit:

Welfare in the here and now
And welfare in a future life.
And because one has realised the good,
The wise person is called a sage.

24 A Heap of Bones

This was said by the Lord . . . .

"Bhikkhus, the skeletons of a single person, running on and wandering in saṁsāra for an aeon, would make a heap of bones, a quantity of bones as large as this Mount Vepulla, if there were someone to collect them and if the collection were not destroyed."

The bones of a single person
Accumulated in a single aeon
Would make a heap like a mountain —
So said the Great Sage.

He declared it to be
As great as Mount Vepulla
To the north of Vulture's Peak
In the hill-fort of Magadha.

But when one sees with perfect wisdom
The four noble truths as they are —
Suffering, the origin of suffering,
The overcoming of suffering,
And the noble eightfold path
Leading to relief from suffering —

Having merely run on
Seven times at the most,
By destroying all fetters
One makes an end of suffering.[27]

25 Lying

This was said by the Lord . . . .

"Bhikkhus, I say that for an individual who transgresses in one thing, there is no evil deed whatsoever he would not do. What is that one thing? It is this, bhikkhus: deliberately telling a lie."

There is no evil that cannot be done
By a person who deliberately lies,
Who transgresses in one thing,
Taking no account of the next world.

26 Giving

This was said by the Lord . . . .

"Bhikkhus, if beings knew, as I know, the result of giving and sharing,[28] they would not eat without having given nor would they allow the stain of meanness to obsess them and take root in their minds. Even if it were their last morsel, their last mouthful, they would not enjoy eating[29] without having shared it, if there were someone to share it with. But, bhikkhus, as beings do not know, as I know, the result of giving and sharing, they eat without having given and the stain of meanness obsesses them and takes root in their minds."

If beings only knew—
So said the Great Sage—
How the result of sharing
Is of such great fruit,
With a gladdened mind,
Rid of the stain of meanness,
They would duly give to noble ones
Who make what is given fruitful.

Having given much food as offering
To those most worthy of offerings,

The donors go to heaven
On departing the human state.
And gone to heaven they rejoice,
And enjoying pleasures there,
The unselfish experience the result
Of generously sharing with others.

27 The Development of Loving-Kindness

This was said by the Lord . . . .

"Bhikkhus, whatever grounds there are for making merit productive of a future birth,[30] all these do not equal a sixteenth part of the mind-release of loving-kindness.[31] The mind-release of loving-kindness surpasses them and shines forth, bright and brilliant.

"Just as the radiance of all the stars does not equal a sixteenth part of the moon's radiance, but the moon's radiance surpasses them and shines forth, bright and brilliant, even so, whatever grounds there are for making merit productive of a future birth, all these do not equal a sixteenth part of the mind-release of loving-kindness . . . .

"Just as in the last month of the rainy season, in the autumn, when the sky is clear and free of clouds, the sun, on ascending, dispels the darkness of space and shines forth, bright and brilliant, even so, whatever grounds there are for making merit productive of a future birth, all these do not equal a sixteenth part of the mind-release of loving-kindness . . . .

"And just as in the night, at the moment of dawn, the morning star shines forth, bright and brilliant, even so, whatever grounds there are for making merit productive of a future birth, all these do not equal a sixteenth part of the mind-release of loving-kindness. The mind-release of loving-kindness surpasses them and shines forth, bright and brilliant."

For one who mindfully develops
Boundless loving-kindness
Seeing the destruction of clinging,
The fetters are worn away.

If with an uncorrupted mind
He pervades just one being
With loving kindly thoughts,
He makes some merit through that.

But a noble one produces
An abundance of merit
By having a compassionate mind
Towards all living beings.[32]

Those royal seers who conquered
The earth crowded with beings
Went about making offerings:
The horse sacrifice, the man sacrifice,
The water rites, the soma sacrifice,
And that called "the Unobstructed."[33]

But these do not share
Even a sixteenth part
Of a mind well cultivated
In loving kindly thoughts,
Just as the entire starry host
Is dimmed by the moon's radiance.

One who does not kill
Nor cause others to kill,
Who does not conquer
Nor cause others to conquer,
Kindly towards all beings—
He has enmity for none.

This too is the meaning of what was said by the Lord, so I heard.

2

THE SECTION OF THE TWOS

28 Living in Discomfort

This was said by the Lord . . . .

"Bhikkhus, possessed of two things, a bhikkhu lives in discomfort here and now, bringing upon himself vexation, trouble and distress, and when the body perishes after death a bad bourn is to be expected. What are the two? Being unguarded regarding the doors of the senses and being immoderate in eating.[1] These are the two things possessed of which a bhikkhu lives in discomfort . . . ."

The eye, ear, nose, tongue,
Body and likewise the mind—
A bhikkhu who leaves these
Doors unguarded here,

Immoderate in eating,
Of uncontrolled senses,
Experiences suffering
Both bodily and mental.

Being tormented by body
And tormented by mind,
Such a one lives in discomfort
Both by day and by night.

29 Living in Comfort

This was said by the Lord . . . .

"Bhikkhus, possessed of two things a bhikkhu lives in

comfort here and now, not bringing upon himself vexation, trouble and distress, and when the body perishes after death a good bourn is to be expected. What are the two? Being guarded regarding the doors of the senses and being moderate in eating. These are the two . . . ."

The eye, ear, nose, tongue,
Body and likewise the mind—
A bhikkhu who has these
Doors well guarded here,

Moderate in eating,
Of controlled senses,
Experiences happiness
Both bodily and mental.

Not tormented by body,
Not tormented by mind,
Such a one lives in comfort
Both by day and by night.

30 Remorse

This was said by the Lord . . . .

"There are two things, bhikkhus, causing remorse. What are the two? Here someone has not done what is good, not done what is wholesome, not done what is beneficial,[2] but has done evil, callous, wrongful deeds. He is remorseful on thinking, 'I have not done good,' and is remorseful on thinking, 'I have done evil.' These, bhikkhus, are the two things causing remorse."

Having performed misconduct
By body, misconduct by speech,
Misconduct by mind and whatever
Else is reckoned a fault—

Not having done a good deed
And done much that is bad —
When his body perishes
That foolish one is reborn in hell.

31 Non-remorse

This was said by the Lord . . . .

"There are two things, bhikkhus, causing no remorse. What are the two? Here someone has done what is good, done what is wholesome, done what is beneficial, and has not done evil, callous, wrongful deeds. He is not remorseful on thinking, 'I have done good,' and is not remorseful on thinking, 'I have done no evil.' These, bhikkhus, are the two things causing no remorse."

Having abandoned misconduct
By body, misconduct by speech,
Misconduct by mind and whatever
Else is reckoned a fault—

Not having done a bad deed
And done much that is good—
When his body perishes
That wise one is reborn in heaven.

32 Behaviour (1)

This was said by the Lord . . . .

"Possessing two things, bhikkhus, a person is placed in hell as if carried there. What are the two things? Possessing bad behaviour and a bad view.[3] These, bhikkhus, are the two things . . . . "

If a person possesses these two things —
Bad behaviour and a bad view —
When his body perishes
That foolish one is reborn in hell.

33 Behaviour (2)

This was said by the Lord . . . .

"Possessing two things, bhikkhus, a person is placed in heaven as if carried there. What are the two things? Possessing good behaviour and a good view. These are the two things . . . ."

If a person possesses these two things —
Good behaviour and a good view —
When his body perishes
That wise one is reborn in heaven.

34 Ardour

This was said by the Lord . . . .

"Bhikkhus, a bhikkhu who is without ardour and without fear of wrongdoing is incapable of attaining enlightenment, incapable of attaining Nibbāna, incapable of attaining the supreme security from bondage. But a bhikkhu who has ardour and fear of wrongdoing is capable of doing so."

One who is not ardent, reckless,
Lazy and of little vigour,
Full of lethargy and torpor,
Shameless and without respect—
Such a bhikkhu cannot attain
Enlightenment which is supreme.

But a mindful and discerning meditator,
Ardent, scrupulous and diligent,
Having severed the fetters of birth and decay,
Can attain for himself right here and now
Enlightenment which is supreme.

35 Not Deceiving (1)

This was said by the Lord . . . .

"Bhikkhus, this holy life is not lived for the sake of deceiving people, for the sake of cajoling people, for the sake of profiting in gain, honour and fame, nor with the idea, 'Let people know me thus.' This holy life, bhikkhus, is lived for the sake of restraint and abandoning."[4]

The Lord taught a holy life
Not based on tradition,[5]
For restraint and abandoning,
Leading to and merging in Nibbāna.

This is the path followed by the great,
Pursued by the lofty sages.
Those who enter that course
As taught by the Enlightened One,
Heeding the Teacher's instruction,
Will make an end of suffering.

36 Not Deceiving (2)

This was said by the Lord . . . .

"Bhikkhus, this holy life is not lived for the sake of deceiving people, for the sake of cajoling people, for the sake of profiting in gain, honour and fame, nor with the idea, 'Let people know me thus.' This holy life, bhikkhus, is lived for the sake of direct knowledge and full understanding."[6]

The Lord taught a holy life
Not based on tradition,
For knowledge and understanding,
Leading to and merging in Nibbāna.

This is the path followed by the great,
Pursued by the lofty sages.
Those who enter that course
As taught by the Enlightened One,
Heeding the Teacher's instructions,
Will make an end of suffering.[7]

37 Happiness

This was said by the Lord . . . .

"Bhikkhus, possessing two things a bhikkhu lives here and now with much pleasure and happiness and is properly motivated for the destruction of the taints.[8] What are the two things? Being moved by a sense of urgency on occasions for urgency, and being moved, making a proper endeavour. These, bhikkhus, are the two things . . . ."[9]

A wise person should be urgently moved
On occasions that make for urgency;
As an ardent discerning bhikkhu
He should investigate with wisdom.

One living ardent thus,
Of peaceful conduct, not proud,
Practising tranquility of mind,
May attain the destruction of suffering.

38 Often Occurring Thoughts

This was said by the Lord . . . .

"Bhikkhus, two thoughts often occur to the Tathāgata,[10] the Arahant, the Fully Enlightened One: the thought of security (for beings) and the thought of solitude.[11]

"The Tathāgata, bhikkhus, is one who delights in and enjoys non-ill will.[12] As the Tathāgata delights in and enjoys non-ill will, this thought often occurs to him: 'By this behaviour I do not oppress anyone either frail or firm.'[13] The Tathāgata, bhikkhus, is one who delights in and enjoys solitude. As the Tathāgata delights in and enjoys solitude, this thought often occurs to him: 'What is unwholesome has been abandoned.'[14]

"Therefore, bhikkhus, I say, you too must live delighting in and enjoying non-ill will. As you so live this thought will often also occur to you: 'By this behaviour we do not oppress anyone either frail or firm.'

"Bhikkhus, you too must live delighting in and enjoying solitude. As you so live this thought will often also occur to you: 'What is unwholesome? What has not been abandoned? What have we abandoned?' "

Two thoughts occur to him,
The Tathāgata, the Awakened One
Who endured that beyond endurance:[15]
Security (for beings) was the first thought
spoken of,
Solitude was the second announced.

The dispeller of darkness, gone beyond,
The great sage who has reached attainment,
Become a master, freed from taints,
Who has crossed over entirely,[16]
Released by the destruction of craving—

That sage bears his final body,
And having left behind Māra,[17] *I say,*
He has gone beyond decay.

As one standing on a mountain peak
Might see all round the people down below,
So having ascended the Dhamma-palace,
The vastly wise, all-seeing one
Views the people of the world.
The sorrowless one views below
Those still immersed in sorrow,
Overwhelmed by birth and decay.[18]

39 Dhamma-teachings

This was said by the Lord . . . .

"There are, bhikkhus, two successive Dhamma-teachings of the Tathāgata, the Arahant, the Fully Enlightened One. What are the two? 'See evil as evil'—this is the first Dhamma-teaching. 'Having seen evil as evil, be rid of it, be detached from it, be freed from it'—this is the second Dhamma-teaching. These, bhikkhus, are the two successive Dhamma-teachings of the Tathāgata . . . . "

Regard the ordered words he spoke,
The Tathāgata, the Awakened One,
Compassionate for all beings,
And the two things he proclaimed:

"See what is evil" is one,
The other "Be detached from it."
With a mind become detached from evil
You will make an end of suffering.

40 Knowledge

This was said by the Lord . . . .

"Ignorance, bhikkhus, precedes and leads to unwholesome things, and shamelessness and lack of fear of wrongdoing follow after. Knowledge, bhikkhus, precedes and leads to wholesome things, and shame and fear of wrongdoing follow after."[19]

Whatever bad bourns there are
In this world and hereafter,
All are rooted in ignorance,
Constructed by desire and greed.

Since one of evil desires is
Shameless and disrespectful,
From that evil flows forth
And he goes to a state of misery.

Thence by discarding desire and greed,
Along with ignorance as well,
A bhikkhu arouses knowledge
And abandons all bad bourns.

41 Deprived of Wisdom

This was said by the Lord . . . .

"Bhikkhus, those beings are thoroughly deprived who are deprived of noble wisdom. They live in discomfort even here and now, with vexation, trouble and distress, and when the body perishes at death a bad bourn is to be expected.

"Those beings are not deprived who are not deprived of noble wisdom. They live in comfort here and now, without vexation, trouble and distress, and when the body perishes at death a good bourn is to be expected."

See the world with its devas,
Destitute of wisdom,
Established in name and form,
Conceiving this to be the truth. [20]

Wisdom which leads to penetration [21]
Is the best thing in the world;
By this one completely understands
The ending of both birth and being.

Devas and human beings hold dear
Those awakened ones ever mindful,
Possessing joyous wisdom,
Bearing their final bodies.

42 The Bright Protectors

This was said by the Lord . . . .

"Bhikkhus, these two bright principles protect the world. What are the two? Shame and fear of wrong-doing.[22] If, bhikkhus, these two bright principles did not protect the world, there would not be discerned respect for mother or maternal aunt or maternal uncle's wife or a teacher's wife or the wives of other honoured persons, and the world would have fallen into promiscuity, as with goats, sheep, chickens, pigs, dogs and jackels. But as these two bright principles protect the world, there is discerned respect for mother . . . and the wives of other honoured persons."

Those in whom shame and fear of wrong
Are not consistently found
Have deviated from the bright root
And are led back to birth and death.

But those in whom shame and fear of wrong
Are consistently ever present,
Peaceful, mature in the holy life,
They put an end to renewal of being.

43 The Not-Born

This was said by the Lord . . . .

"There is, bhikkhus, a not-born, a not-brought-to-being, a not-made, a not-formed.[23] If, bhikkhus, there were not that not-born, not-brought-to-being, not-made, not-formed, no escape would be discerned from what is born, brought-to-being, made, formed. But since there is a not-born, a not-brought-to-being, a not-made, a not-formed, therefore there is discerned an escape from what is born, brought-to-being, made, formed."

The born, come-to-be, produced,
The made, the formed, the unlasting,
Conjoined with decay and death,
A nest of disease, perishable,
Sprung from nutriment and craving's cord —[24]
That is not fit to take delight in.

The escape from that, the peaceful,
Beyond reasoning, everlasting,
The not-born, the unproduced,
The sorrowless state that is void of stain,
The cessation of states linked to suffering,
The stilling of the conditioned—bliss.

44 The Nibbāna-Element

This was said by the Lord . . . .

"Bhikkhus, there are these two Nibbāna-elements.

What are the two? The Nibbāna-element with residue left and the Nibbāna-element with no residue left.

"What, bhikkhus, is the Nibbāna-element with residue left? Here a bhikkhu is an arahant, one whose taints are destroyed,[25] the holy life fulfilled, who has done what had to be done, laid down the burden, attained the goal, destroyed the fetters of being and is completely released through final knowledge. However, his five sense faculties remain unimpaired, by which he still experiences what is agreeable and disagreeable and feels pleasure and pain. It is the extinction of attachment, hate and delusion in him that is called the Nibbāna-element with residue left.[26]

"Now what, bhikkhus, is the Nibbāna-element with no residue left? Here a bhikkhu is an arahant . . . completely released through final knowledge. For him, here in this very life, all that is experienced, not being delighted in, will be extinguished. That, bhikkhus, is called the Nibbāna-element with no residue left.[27]

"These, bhikkhus, are the two Nibbāna-elements."

These two Nibbāna-elements were made known
By the Seeing One, serene[28] *and unattached:*
One is the element seen here and now
With residue, but with the cord of being
destroyed;[29]
The other, having no residue for the future,
Is that wherein all modes of being utterly cease.

Having understood the unconditioned state,
Released in mind with the cord of being
destroyed,
They have attained to the Dhamma-essence.
Delighting in the destruction (of craving),
Those serene ones have abandoned all being.

45 Living in Seclusion

This was said by the Lord . . . .

"Live enjoying seclusion,[30] bhikkhus; live delighting in seclusion, engage in practising inner mental tranquility, not neglecting meditation, possessing insight[31] and frequenting empty places. If you live enjoying seclusion, bhikkhus, . . . and frequenting empty places, one of two fruits is to be expected: final knowledge here and now or, there being some residual defilement, the state of non-returning."

Those of peaceful mind, discerning,
Mindful and given to meditation,
Clearly see things rightly[32]
And long not for sensual pleasures.

Those peaceful ones, delighting in diligence,
Who see fear in negligence,
Are incapable of falling away
And are close to Nibbāna.

46 The Benefits of the Training

This was said by the Lord . . . .

"Bhikkhus, live so as to realise the benefits of the training, the attainment of higher wisdom, the essence of release and the control of mindfulness. Bhikkhus, if you live to realise the benefits of the training . . . one of two fruits is to be expected: final knowledge here and now or, there being some residual defilement, the state of non-returning."

One who has completed the training,
Incapable of falling away,
Attained to the higher wisdom,

A seer of the end of birth —
That sage bears his final body,
And having left behind conceit,
He has gone beyond decay, I say.

Therefore ever delighting in meditation,
Concentrated, with ardent energy,
Seeing the end of birth, O bhikkhus,
Conquer Māra and his host,[33]
And go beyond all birth and death.

47 Vigilance

This was said by the Lord . . . .

"Bhikkhus, a bhikkhu should be vigilant; he should live mindful, clearly comprehending, concentrated, happy and calm, and should know when it is suitable to cultivate those things that are wholesome.[34] Bhikkhus, for a bhikkhu who is vigilant and living thus, one of two fruits is to be expected: final knowledge here and now or, there being some residual defilement, the state of non-returning."

You vigilant ones hear this:
Wake up, you who are asleep!
Vigilance is better than sleep;
There is no fear for the vigilant.

One who is vigilant and mindful,
Comprehending and concentrated,
Joyful and calm in his thoughts,
By rightly investigating the Dhamma
With unified mind, will in time
Destroy the darkness of ignorance.

Therefore be devoted to vigilance,
An ardent, discerning, meditative bhikkhu.
Having severed the fetter of birth and decay,
One may here and now attain
Enlightenment which is supreme.

48 A State of Misery

This was said by the Lord . . . .

"Bhikkhus, these two will go to a state of misery, to hell, by not giving up such conduct as this. What two? One who while no liver of the holy life pretends to be one who lives the holy life, and one who falsely accuses another who lives the holy life in complete purity of not living it. These two will go to a state of misery, to hell, by not giving up such conduct as this."

The false-accuser goes to hell
And also one who denies the deed he did,
Both these become equal hereafter,
Persons of base actions in the world beyond.

Many imposters wear the yellow robe
Though evil-natured and uncontrolled.
Because of their evil deeds,
Those evil ones are born in hell.

Far better for him to swallow
A fiery hot iron ball
Than that immoral and uncontrolled
He should eat the country's alms.[35]

49 Held by Views

This was said by the Lord . . . .

"Bhikkhus, held by two kinds of views, some devas

and men hold back and some overreach; only those with vision see.

"And how, bhikkhus, do some hold back? Devas and men enjoy being, delight in being, are satisfied with being. When Dhamma is taught to them for the cessation of being,[36] their minds do not enter into it or acquire confidence in it or settle upon it or become resolved upon it. Thus, bhikkhus, do some hold back.[37]

"How, bhikkhus, do some overreach? Now some are troubled, ashamed and disgusted by this very same being and they rejoice in (the idea of) non-being, asserting: 'In as much as this self, good sirs, when the body perishes at death, is annihilated and destroyed and does not exist after death—this is peaceful, this is excellent, this is reality!' Thus, bhikkhus, do some overreach.[38]

"How, bhikkhus, do those with vision see? Herein a bhikkhu sees what has come to be as having come to be. Having seen it thus, he practises the course for turning away, for dispassion, for the cessation of what has come to be. Thus, bhikkhus, do those with vision see."[39]

Having seen what has come to be
As having come to be,
Passing beyond what has come to be,
They are released in accordance with truth
By exhausting the craving for being.

When a bhikkhu has fully understood,
That which has come to be as such,
Free from craving to be this or that,
By the extinction of what has come to be
He comes no more to renewal of being.

This too is the meaning of what was said by the Lord, so I heard.

3

THE SECTION OF THE THREES

50 Roots

This was said by the Lord . . . .

"Bhikkhus, there are these three unwholesome roots. What three? The unwholesome root greed, the unwholesome root hate, the unwholesome root delusion. These are the three."

Greed and hate and delusion,
Arisen from within himself,
Harm an evil-minded person
As its own fruit destroys
The growth of the bamboo tree.[1]

51 Elements

This was said by the Lord . . . .

"Bhikkhus, there are these three elements. What three? The form element, the formless element and the element of cessation.[2] These are the three."

By fully understanding the form element
Without getting stuck in the formless,
They are released into cessation
And leave Death far behind them.[3]

Having touched with his own person[4]
The deathless element free from clinging,
Having realised the relinquishment

Of clinging, his taints all gone,
The Fully Enlightened One proclaims
The sorrowless state that is void of stain.

52 Feelings (1)

This was said by the Lord . . . .

"Bhikkhus, there are these three feelings. What three? Pleasant feeling, painful feeling and neither-pleasant-nor-painful feeling. These are the three."

A disciple of the Buddha,
Concentrated, clearly comprehending
And mindful, knows feelings
And the origin of feelings,
Where they cease and the path
That leads to their full destruction.[5]
With the destruction of feelings a bhikkhu,
Without longing, has attained Nibbāna.

53 Feelings (2)

This was said by the Lord . . . .

"Bhikkhus, there are these three feelings. What three? Pleasant feeling, painful feeling and neither-pleasant-nor-painful feeling. Pleasant feeling, bhikkhus, should be seen as suffering,[6] painful feeling should be seen as a dart, neither-pleasant-nor-painful feeling should be seen as impermanent.

"When, bhikkhus, a bhikkhu has seen these three feelings thus, he is said to be a noble one who sees rightly. He has cut off craving, destroyed the fetters, and by thoroughly understanding conceit, he has made an end of suffering."

One sees pleasure as suffering
And sees pain as a dart.
One sees as impermanent the peaceful feeling
That is neither pleasant nor painful.

Such a bhikkhu who sees rightly
Is thereby well released.
Accomplished in knowledge, at peace,
That sage has overcome all bonds.

54 Search (1)

This was said by the Lord . . . .

"Bhikkhus, there are these three kinds of search.[7] What three? The search for sensual gratification, the search for being, the search for a holy life.[8] These are the three."

A disciple of the Buddha,
Concentrated, clearly comprehending
And mindful, knows searches
And the origin of searches,
Where they cease and the path
That leads to their full destruction.
With the destruction of searches a bhikkhu,
Without longing, has attained Nibbāna.

55 Search (2)

This was said by the Lord . . . .

"Bhikkhus, there are these three kinds of search. . . ."

Sensual search, the search for being,
The search for a holy life of one
Who takes his stand upon a view

And holds it tightly as the truth—
These are heapings of defilements.

For a bhikkhu wholly dispassionate
And freed by the destruction of craving,
Searches have been relinquished
And uprooted the standpoint of views.
With the destruction of searches a bhikkhu
Is free from desire and doubt.

56 Taints (1)

This was said by the Lord . . . .

"Bhikkhus, there are these three taints. What three? The taint of sensual desire, the taint of being, the taint of ignorance. These are the three."

A disciple of the Buddha,
Concentrated, clearly comprehending
And mindful, knows the taints
And the origin of taints,
Where they cease and the path
That leads to their full destruction.
With the destruction of the taints a bhikkhu,
Without longing, has attained Nibbāna.

57 Taints (2)

This was said by the Lord . . . .

"Bhikkhus, there are these three taints . . . ."

One for whom the taint of desire
For sensual pleasures has been destroyed,
Who has eliminated ignorance
And exhausted the taint of being—
Such a one is released without clinging.
Having conquered Māra and his mount,[9]
He bears his final body.

58 Craving

This was said by the Lord . . . .

"Bhikkhus, there are these three cravings. What three? The craving for sensual pleasures, the craving for being, the craving for non-being. These are the three."

Those fettered by the bond of craving,
Whose minds delight in being this or that,
Are people in the bondage of Māra
Who enjoy no security from bondage.
Such beings continue in saṁsāra,
Going on from birth to death.

But those who have abandoned craving,
Free from craving for being this or that,
Having attained the taints' destruction,
Though in the world, have gone beyond.

59 Māra's Domain

This was said by the Lord . . . .

"Bhikkhus, being in possession of three things, a bhikkhu has passed beyond the domain of Māra[10] and shines like the sun. What are the three? Herein a bhikkhu is in possession of the non-learner's[11] aggregate of virtue, the non-learner's aggregate of concentration, the non-learner's aggregate of wisdom.[12] These are the three things in possession of which a bhikkhu has passed beyond the domain of Māra and shines like the sun."

Virtue, concentration and wisdom —
One in whom these are fully developed,
On passing beyond Māra's domain,
Shines forth like the sun.

60 Grounds for Making Merit

This was said by the Lord . . . .

"Bhikkhus, there are these three grounds for making merit. What three? The ground for making merit consisting in giving, the ground for making merit consisting in virtue, the ground for making merit consisting in mind-development. These are the three."

One should train in deeds of merit
That yield long-lasting happiness:
Generosity, a balanced life,
Developing a loving mind.

By cultivating these three things,
Deeds yielding happiness,
The wise person is reborn in bliss
In an untroubled happy world. [13]

61 Eyes

This was said by the Lord . . . .

"Bhikkhus, there are these three eyes. What three? The fleshly eye, the divine eye and the wisdom eye.[14] These, bhikkhus, are the three eyes."

The fleshly eye, the divine eye
And the unsurpassed wisdom eye—
These three eyes were described
By the Buddha, supreme among men.

The arising of the fleshly eye
Is the path to the divine eye, [15]
But the unsurpassed wisdom eye
Is that from which knowledge arises.
By obtaining such an eye
One is released from all suffering. [16]

62 Faculties

This was said by the Lord . . . .

"Bhikkhus, there are these three faculties.[17] What three? The faculty of the assurance: 'I shall come to finally know what is as yet not finally known'; the faculty of final knowledge; the faculty of one who has finally known.[18] These, bhikkhus, are the three faculties."

For a learner who is training
In conformity with the direct path,[19]
The knowledge of destruction arises first,
And final knowledge immediately follows.[20]

Freed by that final knowledge,
By destroying the fetters of being
The serene one has the certainty:
"Unshakable is my release."

Endowed with this faculty
The peaceful one delights in the peaceful
state.[21]
Having conquered Māra and his mount,
He bears his final body.

63 Time

This was said by the Lord . . . .

"Bhikkhus, these are the three times. What three? Past time, future time and present time. These, bhikkhus, are the three times."

Perceiving what can be expressed through concepts,
Beings take their stand on what is expressed.[22]
Not fully understanding the expressed,
They come under the bondage of Death.

But by fully understanding what is expressed
One does not misconceive the speaker.[23]
His mind has attained to freedom,
The unsurpassed state of peace.

Understanding what is expressed,
The peaceful one delights in the peaceful state.
Standing on Dhamma,[24] *perfect in knowledge,*
He freely makes use of concepts
But no more enters into concept's range.[25]

64 Misconduct

This was said by the Lord . . . .

"Bhikkhus, there are these three kinds of misconduct. What are the three? Misconduct by body, misconduct by speech and misconduct by mind. These are the three."

Having performed misconduct
By body, misconduct by speech,
Misconduct by mind and whatever
Else is reckoned a fault —

Not having done a good deed
And done much that is bad —
When his body perishes
That foolish one is reborn in hell.[26]

65 Good Conduct

This was said by the Lord . . . .

"Bhikkhus, there are these three kinds of good conduct. What are the three? Good conduct by body, good conduct by speech and good conduct by mind. These are the three."

Having abandoned misconduct
By body, misconduct by speech,
Misconduct by mind and whatever
Else is reckoned a fault—

Not having done a bad deed
And done much that is good—
When his body perishes
That wise one is reborn in heaven.

66 Purity

This was said by the Lord . . . .

"Bhikkhus, there are these three kinds of purity. What are the three? Purity of body, purity of speech and purity of mind. These are the three."

Bodily pure, pure of speech,
Mentally pure and taintless—
A pure one possessing such purity
Is called one who has abandoned all.

67 Perfection

This was said by the Lord . . . .

"Bhikkhus, there are these three kinds of perfection. What are the three? Perfection of body, perfection of speech and perfection of mind. These are the three."

Bodily perfect, perfect of speech,
Mentally perfect and taintless;
A sage possessing such perfection [27]
Is called one cleansed of evil.

68 Attachment (1)

This was said by the Lord . . . .

"Bhikkhus, in whomsoever attachment is not abandoned, hate is not abandoned, delusion is not abandoned, this person is said to be in the bondage of Māra; he is caught in Māra's noose and at the mercy of the Evil One.

"Bhikkhus, in whomsoever attachment is abandoned, hate is abandoned, delusion is abandoned, this person is said to be free from the bondage of Māra; he has cast off Māra's noose and is not at the mercy of the Evil One."

One who has destroyed attachment
Along with hate and ignorance
Is called one inwardly developed,[28]
A Tathāgata become supreme,[29]
Awakened, past enmity and fear,
One who has abandoned all.

69 Attachment (2)

This was said by the Lord . . . .

"Bhikkhus, in whatsoever bhikkhu or bhikkhunī attachment is not abandoned, hate is not abandoned, delusion is not abandoned, this person is said to be one who has not crossed the ocean with its waves, breakers and eddies, its sharks and demons.[30] But in whatsoever bhikkhu or bhikkhunī attachment is abandoned, hate is abandoned, delusion is abandoned, that person is said to be one who has crossed the ocean with its waves, breakers and eddies, its sharks and demons—one of whom it is said: 'Crossed over, gone beyond, the brahmin stands on dry ground.'"[31]

One who has destroyed attachment
Along with hate and ignorance
Has crossed this ocean
With its sharks and demons,
Its fearful waves so hard to cross.

He has surmounted every tie,
Left Death behind,
Become free from clinging,
Forsaken suffering and renewal of being.
Vanished, he cannot be defined, I say—
He has bewildered the King of Death.[32]

70 Wrong View

This was said by the Lord . . . .

"Bhikkhus, I have seen beings who practise misconduct by body, speech and mind, who vilify the noble ones, hold wrong view and perform various deeds because of their wrong view. Those beings, when the body perishes, are reborn after death in a state of misery, a bad bourn, a state of ruin, in hell. I say this, bhikkhus, without having learned it from another recluse or brahmin.[33] It is just because I myself have known it, seen it and observed it that I say: 'Bhikkhus, I have seen beings who practise misconduct by body, speech and mind . . . reborn after death in a state of misery . . . in hell.' "

An individual here with
A wrongly directed mind
Who utters wrong speech
And performs wrong deeds,
One of little learning,
Who does demerit in this short life —
Upon the perishing of the body
That foolish one is reborn in hell.

71 Right View

This was said by the Lord . . . .

"Bhikkhus, I have seen beings who practise good conduct by body, speech and mind, who do not vilify the noble ones, who hold right view and who perform various deeds because of their right view. Those beings, when the body perishes, are reborn after death in a good bourn, a heavenly world. I say this, bhikkhus, without having learned it from another recluse or brahmin. It is just because I myself have known it, seen it and observed it that I say: 'Bhikkhus, I have seen beings who practise good conduct by body, speech and mind . . . reborn after death in a good bourn, a heavenly world.' "

An individual here with
A rightly directed mind
Who utters right speech
And performs right deeds,
One of much learning,
Who does much merit in this short life —
Upon the perishing of the body
That wise one is reborn in heaven.

72 Escape

This was said by the Lord . . . .

"Bhikkhus, there are these three elements of escape. What three? The escape from sensual desires, that is, renunciation; the escape from form, that is, the formless; and the escape from whatever has come to be, is conditioned and dependently arisen, that is, cessation.[34] These, bhikkhus, are the three elements of escape."

Having known the escape from sensual desires
And the overcoming of forms,
One whose energy is always ardent
Reaches the stilling of all formations.[35]

Such a bhikkhu who sees rightly
Is thereby well released.
Accomplished in knowledge, at peace,
That sage has overcome all bonds.[36]

73 More Peaceful

This was said by the Lord . . . .

"Bhikkhus, the formless is more peaceful than the form realm and cessation is more peaceful than the formless."

Those beings who reach the form realm
And those established in the formless,
If they do not know cessation
Come back to renewal of being.

Those who fully understand forms
Without getting stuck in the formless,
Are released into cessation
And leave Death far behind them.

Having touched with his own person
The deathless element free from clinging,
Having realised the relinquishment
Of clinging, his taints all gone,
The Fully Enlightened One proclaims
The sorrowless state that is void of stain.[37]

74 Sons

This was said by the Lord . . . .

"Bhikkhus, these three kinds of sons are found existing in the world. What three? The superior kind, the similar kind and the inferior kind.

"Now what, bhikkhus, is the superior kind of son? In this instance a son has a mother and father who have not gone for refuge to the Buddha, to the Dhamma, and to the Sangha; who do not abstain from taking life, from taking what has not been given, from wrong conduct in sensual desires, from false speech, and from intoxicating drink leading to negligence;[38] who are unvirtuous and of bad conduct. But the son is one who has gone for refuge to the Buddha, to the Dhamma, and to the Sangha; who abstains from taking life, from taking what has not been given, from wrong conduct in sensual desires, from false speech, and from intoxicating drink leading to negligence; who is virtuous and of good conduct. This, bhikkhus, is the superior kind of son.

"Now what, bhikkhus, is the similar kind of son? In this instance a son has a mother and father who have gone for refuge to the Buddha . . . ; who abstain from taking life . . . ; who are virtuous and of good conduct. And the son also is one who has gone for refuge to the Buddha . . . ; who abstains from taking life . . . ; who is virtuous and of good conduct. This, bhikkhus, is the similar kind of son.

"Now what, bhikkhus, is the inferior kind of son? In this instance a son has a mother and father who have gone for refuge to the Buddha . . . ; who abstain from taking life . . . ; who are virtuous and of good conduct. But the son is one who has not gone for refuge to the Buddha . . . ; who does not abstain from taking life . . . ; who is unvirtuous and of bad conduct. This, bhikkhus, is the inferior kind of son.

"These, bhikkhus, are the three kinds of sons found existing in the world."

The wise wish for a son
Who is superior or similar.
They do not wish for one
Who is inferior, who will be
A disgrace to the family.

But such sons in the world like these
Who are devoted lay-followers,
Excelling in faith and virtue,
Liberal, without selfishness,
Shine forth in assemblies
Like the moon freed from clouds.

75 A Rainless Cloud

This was said by the Lord . . . .

"Bhikkhus, these three kinds of persons are to be found existing in the world. What three? One who is like a rainless cloud, one who rains locally and one who rains everywhere.

"Now what kind of person, bhikkhus, is like a rainless cloud? Here, a certain person is not a giver to anyone; he does not give food, drink, clothing, vehicles, garlands, scents, ointments, beds, lodging and lamps to recluses and brahmins, to the poor, destitute and needy. This kind of person is like a rainless cloud.

"Now what, bhikkhus, is the kind of person who rains locally? Here, a certain person is a giver to some but not a giver to others. Food, drink, clothing, vehicles, garlands, scents, ointments, beds, lodging and lamps he gives only to some recluses and brahmins, to some of the poor, destitute and needy, but not to others. This is the kind of person who rains locally.

"Now what, bhikkhus, is the kind of person who rains everywhere? Here, a certain person gives to all. He gives food, drink, clothing, vehicles, garlands, scents, ointments, beds, lodging and lamps to all recluses and brahmins, to the poor, destitute and needy. This is the kind of person who rains everywhere.

"These, bhikkhus, are the three kinds of persons to be found existing in the world."

Neither to recluses nor brahmins
Nor to the poor and destitute
Does he distribute his store
Of food and drink and goods;
That base person is called
"One like a rainless cloud."

To some he does not give,
To some he does offer alms;
That one wise people call
"One who rains only locally."

A person renowned for his plenty,
Compassionate towards all beings,
Distributes alms gladly.
"Give! Give!" he says.[39]

Like a great storm cloud
That thunders and rains down
Filling the levels and hollows,
Saturating the earth with water,
Even so is such a person.

Having righteously gathered wealth
Which he obtains by his own effort,
He fully satisfies with food and drink
Whatever beings must live in need.

76 Aspiring for Happiness

This was said by the Lord . . . .

"Bhikkhus, aspiring for these three kinds of happiness, a wise person should guard virtuous conduct.

What are the three? Aspiring 'May praise come to me,' a wise person should guard virtuous conduct. Aspiring 'May I become wealthy,' a wise person should guard virtuous conduct. Aspiring 'Upon the perishing of the body at death may I be reborn in a good bourn, a heavenly world,' a wise person should guard virtuous conduct. These are the three kinds of happiness aspiring for which a wise person should guard virtuous conduct."

Aspiring for three kinds of happiness
The wise person should guard virtue:
Praise, the obtaining of property,
Rejoicing in heaven hereafter.

If one who does no evil
Associates with an evil-doer,
He is suspected of evil
And his disrepute grows.

Whatever person is made a friend,
Whomever one associates with,
One becomes of like quality,
One becomes like one's companion.

The follower and the followed,
One who contacts and one contacted,
Are like an arrow coated with poison
That contaminates the quiver it is in.
Fearing contamination the wise person
Should not have evil friends.

A man who ties up putrid fish
With some blades of kusa-grass
Makes the kusa-grass smell putrid;
So it is with those who follow fools.

But a man who wraps tagara powder[40]
In the broad leaf of a tree
Makes the leaf smell fragrant;
So it is with those who follow sages.

Therefore as with the leaf-container,
Understanding the outcome for oneself,
The unvirtuous should not be followed,
A wise person should follow the virtuous.
The unvirtuous lead one to hell,
The virtuous help one reach heaven.

77 Perishable

This was said by the Lord . . . .

"This body, bhikkhus, is perishable, consciousness is of a nature to dissolve, and all objects of clinging are impermanent, suffering and subject to change."

Having known the body as perishable
And consciousness as bound to dissolve,
Having seen the fear in objects of clinging,
He has gone beyond birth and death;
Having attained supreme peace,
With composed mind he bides his time.

78 Like Elements

This was said by the Lord . . . .

"Bhikkhus, it is according to like elements that beings associate with each other and come together.[41] Beings of low disposition associate and come together with beings of low disposition. Beings of good disposition associate and come together with beings of good disposition. It was so in the past, it will be so in the future, and it is so in the present."

Desire born of association
Is severed by non-association.
As one riding on a wooden plank
Would sink in the mighty ocean,

Even so one of virtuous life
Sinks by consorting with an idler.
Therefore shun an idle person,
One who makes little effort.
Live with those who dwell secluded,
The noble ones resolved and meditative,
Who are ever strenuous and wise.

79 Falling Away

This was said by the Lord . . . .

"Three things, bhikkhus, lead to the falling away of a learner bhikkhu. What are the three? Here, a learner bhikkhu enjoys activity,[42] is fond of activity, enjoys indulging in activity. He enjoys gossip, is fond of gossip, enjoys indulging in gossip. He enjoys sleep, is fond of sleep, enjoys indulging in sleep. These are the three things that lead to the falling away of a learner bhikkhu.

"Three things, bhikkhus, protect a learner bhikkhu from falling away. What are the three? Here, a learner bhikkhu does not enjoy activity, is not fond of activity, does not enjoy indulging in activity. He does not enjoy gossip, is not fond of gossip, does not enjoy indulging in gossip. He does not enjoy sleep, is not fond of sleep, does not enjoy indulging in sleep. These are the three things that protect a learner bhikkhu from falling away."

A bhikkhu who enjoys activity,
Restless, fond of gossip and sleep,
Will never be able to attain
Enlightenment which is supreme.

Thus let him restrict his duties,
Give up sloth and restlessness;
Such a bhikkhu can attain
Enlightenment which is supreme.

80 Unwholesome Thoughts

This was said by the Lord . . . .

"Bhikkhus, there are these three kinds of unwholesome thoughts. What three? A thought concerned with not being despised;[43] a thought concerned with gain, honour and fame; a thought concerned with involvement in the affairs of others.[44] These, bhikkhus, are the three kinds of unwholesome thoughts."

One concerned with not being despised,
With gain, honour and esteem,
And who delights in companionship
Is far from the destruction of fetters.

But having abandoned sons and herds,
Family life and his possessions,
Such a bhikkhu can attain
Enlightenment which is supreme.

81 Homage

This was said by the Lord . . . .

"Bhikkhus, I have seen beings, overwhelmed and with minds obsessed by receiving homage, upon the perishing of the body after death be reborn in a state of misery, a bad bourn, a state of ruin, hell. I have seen beings, overwhelmed and with minds obsessed by not receiving homage . . . by both receiving homage and (later) not receiving homage, upon the perishing of the body after death be reborn in a state of misery, a bad bourn, a state of ruin, hell.

"I say this, bhikkhus, without having learned it from another recluse or brahmin . . . . It is just because I myself have known it, seen it and observed it, that I say: I have seen beings, overwhelmed and with minds obsessed by receiving homage . . . after death be reborn in . . . hell."

He is one who lives diligently
With concentration undisturbed,
Both when homage is paid to him
And when he receives no homage.

Meditating continuously, gifted
With subtle view and insight,
Enjoying the destruction of grasping—
They call such a one a "true man."

82 Joyous Utterances

This was said by the Lord . . . .

"Bhikkhus, among the devas these three joyous utterances are proclaimed from time to time upon certain occasions. What three?

"At the time when a noble disciple, having had his hair and beard shaved off and having clothed himself in the yellow robe, intends going forth from home into homelessness, at that time among the devas the joyous utterance is proclaimed: 'A noble disciple intends to do battle with Māra.' This is the first joyous utterance proclaimed among the devas from time to time upon a certain occasion.

"Again, bhikkhus, at the time when a noble disciple lives engaged in cultivating the seven groups of the requisites of enlightenment,[45] at that time among the devas the joyous utterance is proclaimed: 'A noble disciple is doing battle with Māra.' This is the second joyous utterance proclaimed among the devas from time to time upon a certain occasion.

"And again, bhikkhus, at the time when a noble disciple, through realisation by his own direct knowledge, here and now enters and abides in the mind-release and wisdom-release that are taintless by the destruction of the taints,[46] at that time among the devas the joyous utterance is proclaimed: 'A noble disciple has won the battle. He was in the forefront of the fight and now dwells victorious.' This, bhikkhus, is the third joyous utterance proclaimed among the devas from time to time upon a certain occasion.

"These, bhikkhus, are the three joyous utterances. . . ."

On seeing that he has won the battle,
Even the devas honour him,
The Fully Enlightened One's disciple,
A great one free from diffidence:

"We salute you, O thoroughbred man,
You who have won a difficult conquest.
Having routed the army of Death,
You are unhindered in liberation."

Thus do the devas extoll him,
The one who has attained the goal,
For they do not perceive in him
Ground for subjection to Death's control.[47]

83 The Five Prognostic Signs

This was said by the Lord . . . .

"Bhikkhus, when a deva is due to pass away from a company of devas, five prognostic signs appear: his flower-garlands wither, his clothes become soiled, sweat is released from his armpits, his bodily radiance fades, and the deva takes no delight in his heavenly throne. The devas, observing the prognostic signs that this deva is due to pass away, encourage him in three things with the words: 'Go from here, friend, to a good bourn. Having gone to a good bourn, gain that which is good to gain. Having gained that which is good to gain, become firmly established in it.'"

When this was said, a certain bhikkhu asked the Lord: "Venerable sir, what is reckoned by the devas to be a good bourn? What is reckoned by the devas to be a gain that is good to gain? What is reckoned by the devas to be firmly established?"

"It is human existence, bhikkhus, that is reckoned by the devas to be a good bourn. When a human being acquires faith in the Dhamma-and-discipline taught by the Tathāgata, this is reckoned by the devas to be a gain that is good to gain. When faith is steadfast in him, firmly rooted, established and strong, not to be destroyed[48] by any recluse or brahmin or deva or māra or brahmā or by anyone else in the world, this is reckoned by the devas to be firmly established."

When a deva whose life is exhausted
Passes away from a deva-company,
The devas encourage him
In three ways with the words:

"Go, friend, to a good bourn,
To the fellowship of humans.
On becoming human acquire faith
Unsurpassed in the true Dhamma.

That faith made steadfast,
Become rooted and standing firm,
Will be unshakable for life
In the true Dhamma well proclaimed.

Having abandoned misconduct by body,
Misconduct by speech as well,
Misconduct by mind and whatever else
Is reckoned as a fault,

Having done much that is good
Both by body and by speech,
And done good with a mind
That is boundless and free from clinging,

With that merit as a basis [49]
Made abundant by generosity,
You should establish other people
In the true Dhamma and the holy life."

When the devas know that a deva
Is about to pass from their midst,
Out of compassion they encourage him:
"Return here, deva, again and again."

84 For the Welfare of Many

This was said by the Lord . . . .

"Bhikkhus, these three persons appearing in the world appear for the welfare of many people, for the happiness of many people, out of compassion for the world, for the good, welfare and happiness of devas and humans. What three?

"Here, bhikkhus, a Tathāgata appears in the world, an arahant, a Fully Enlightened One, possessing perfect knowledge and conduct, a sublime one, a world-knower, an unsurpassed leader of men to be tamed, a teacher of devas and humans, an enlightened one, a Lord. He teaches Dhamma that is good at the outset, good in the middle and good at the end, with its correct meaning and wording, and he proclaims the holy life in its fulfilment and complete purity. This, bhikkhus, is the first person appearing in the world who appears for the welfare of many people, for the happiness of many people, out of compassion for the world, for the good, welfare and happiness of devas and humans.

"Next, bhikkhus, there is that teacher's disciple who is an arahant, one whose taints are destroyed, the holy life fulfilled, who has done what had to be done, laid down the burden, attained the goal, destroyed the fetters of being and is completely released through final knowledge. He teaches Dhamma . . . and he proclaims the holy life in its fulfilment and complete purity. This, bhikkhus, is the second person appearing in the world . . . for the good, welfare and happiness of devas and humans.

"And next, bhikkhus, there is a disciple of that teacher, a learner who is following the path, who has learned much and is of virtuous conduct. He teaches Dhamma . . . and he proclaims the holy life in its fulfilment and complete purity. This, bhikkhus, is the third person appearing in the world . . . for the good, welfare and happiness of devas and humans.

"These, bhikkhus, are the three persons appearing in the world who appear for the welfare of many people, for the happiness of many people, out of compassion for the world, for the good, welfare and happiness of devas and humans."

The teacher, the great sage,
Is the first in the world;
Following him is the disciple
Whose composure is perfected;
And then the learner training
On the path, one who has
Learned much and is virtuous.

These three are chief
Amongst devas and humans:
Illuminators, preaching Dhamma,
Opening the door to the Deathless,
They free many people from bondage.

Those who follow the path
Well taught by the unsurpassed
Caravan-leader, who are diligent
In the Sublime One's dispensation,
Make an end of suffering
Within this very life itself.

85 Contemplating Foulness

This was said by the Lord . . . .

"Bhikkhus, live contemplating the foulness in the body.[50] Let mindfulness of breathing be inwardly well established before you. Live contemplating the impermanence of all formations.

"For those who live contemplating foulness in the body, the tendency to lust with regard to the element of beauty is abandoned. When mindfulness of breathing is inwardly well established before one, the tendencies of extraneous thoughts to produce vexation of mind remain no more.[51] For those who live contemplating the impermanence of all formations, ignorance is abandoned and knowledge arises."

Contemplating foulness in the body,
Being mindful of in-and-out breathing,
Ever ardent and seeing clearly
The calming down of all formations;

Such a bhikkhu who sees rightly
Is thereby well released.
Accomplished in knowledge, at peace,
That sage has overcome all bonds.

86 Practice According to Dhamma

This was said by the Lord . . . .

"When referring to a bhikkhu who practises according to Dhamma, this is the proper way of defining 'practice according to Dhamma.' When speaking he speaks only Dhamma, not non-Dhamma. When thinking he thinks only thoughts of Dhamma, not thoughts of non-Dhamma. By avoiding these two [52] he lives with equanimity, mindful and clearly comprehending."

A bhikkhu enjoying the Dhamma
And delighting in the Dhamma,
Reflecting upon the Dhamma,
Does not fall from the true Dhamma.

Whether walking or standing,
Sitting or lying down,
With mind inwardly restrained,
He attains to lasting peace.

87 Producing Blindness

This was said by the Lord . . . .

"Bhikkhus, these three kinds of unwholesome thoughts produce blindness, lack of vision and absence of knowledge; they obstruct wisdom, lead to vexation and are not conducive to Nibbāna. What are the three? A sensual thought, a thought of ill will and an aggressive thought. These, bhikkhus, are the three kinds of unwholesome thoughts that produce blindness . . . and are not conducive to Nibbāna.

"Bhikkhus, these three kinds of wholesome thoughts remove blindness and produce vision, knowledge and the growth of wisdom; they do not lead to vexation and are conducive to Nibbāna. What are the three? A thought of renunciation, a thought of friendliness[53] and a thought of harmlessness. These, bhikkhus, are the three kinds of wholesome thoughts that remove blindness . . . and are conducive to Nibbāna."

Three wholesome thoughts should be entertained,
Three unwholesome thoughts rejected.
One who stops such trains of thoughts
As a shower settles a cloud of dust,
With a mind that has quelled such thoughts
Attains in this life the state of peace.

88 Inner Stains

This was said by the Lord . . . .

"Bhikkhus, these three are inner stains, inner enemies, inner foes, inner murderers, inner adversaries. What three? Greed, bhikkhus, is an inner stain . . . an inner adversary. Hate is an inner stain . . . an inner adversary. Delusion is an inner stain . . . an inner adversary. These are the three."[54]

Greed is a cause of misfortune,
Greed agitates the mind;
People do not understand that as
A danger produced from within.

A greedy person does not know the good,
A greedy person does not see the Dhamma;
Blinding darkness then prevails
When greed overwhelms a man.

But one who has abandoned greed
Longs not for what invites cupidity.
Greed slips away from him
As a water drop from a lotus leaf.

Hate is a cause of misfortune,
Hate agitates the mind;
People do not understand that as
A danger produced from within.

A hater does not know the good,
A hater does not see the Dhamma;
Blinding darkness then prevails
When hate overwhelms a man.

But one who has abandoned hate
Is not angered by what incites to anger.
Hate drops away from him
As a palmyra fruit from its stalk.

Delusion is a cause of misfortune,
Delusion agitates the mind;
People do not understand that as
A danger produced from within.

One deluded does not know the good,
One deluded does not see the Dhamma;
Blinding darkness then prevails
When delusion overwhelms a man.

But one who has abandoned delusion
Is not bewildered by confusing things.
He puts an end to all delusion
As the sunrise puts an end to the dark.

89 Devadatta

This was said by the Lord . . . .

"Bhikkhus, overcome with his mind obsessed by three kinds of wickedness, Devadatta will inevitably go to a state of misery, to hell, for the duration of the aeon.[55] What are the three? Overcome with his mind obsessed by evil desires . . . ; overcome with his mind obsessed by evil friends . . . ; and although there was more that should have been done, he stopped halfway through gaining a trifling attainment of distinction.[56] These, bhikkhus, are the three.

Surely no one of evil desires
Is born again in this world.
Know that he goes to the bourn of those
Who live in the grip of evil desires.

I heard how Devadatta was
Regarded as a wise man,
One developed in meditation
Who shone as it were with fame.

Having thought himself his equal,[57]
He assaulted the Tathāgata
And went to the four-doored frightful place,
Avīci the Unremitting Hell.[58]

When one plots against an innocent
Who has done no evil deed,
That evil merely affects the one
Corrupt of mind and disrespectful.

One who thinks he could pollute
The ocean with a pot of poison
Would not be able to pollute it—
Awesome is that mass of water.

It is similar in attacking with abuse
The Tathāgata who has reached perfection
And ever dwells with peaceful mind—
Abuse has no effect on him.

A wise man should befriend such a one
And constantly follow after him.
A bhikkhu who goes along his path
Can reach the end of suffering.

90 Foremost Faith

This was said by the Lord . . . .

"Bhikkhus, there are these three foremost kinds of faith.[59] What are the three?

"Whatever beings there are, bhikkhus, whether footless or two-footed or four-footed or many-footed, with form or without form, percipient or non-percipient or neither-percipient-nor-non-percipient, of these the Tathāgata is reckoned foremost, the Arahant, the Fully Enlightened One. Those who have faith in the Buddha have faith in the foremost, and for those with faith in the foremost the result will be foremost.[60]

"Whatever states[61] there are, bhikkhus, whether conditioned or unconditioned, of these detachment is reckoned foremost, that is, the subduing of vanity, the elimination of thirst, the removal of reliance, the termination of the round (of rebirths), the destruction of craving, detachment, cessation, Nibbāna. Those who have faith in the Dhamma of detachment have faith in the foremost, and for those with faith in the foremost the result will be foremost.

"Whatever communities or groups there are, bhikkhus, of these the Sangha of the Tathāgata's disciples is reckoned foremost, that is, the four pairs of persons, the eight individuals.[62] This Sangha of the Lord's disciples is worthy of gifts, worthy of hospitality, worthy of offerings, worthy of reverential salutation, the unsurpassable field of merit for the world. Those who have faith in the Sangha have faith in the foremost, and for those with faith in the foremost the result will be foremost.

"These, bhikkhus, are the three foremost kinds of faith."

This is foremost for those with faith,
For those who know the foremost Dhamma:
Having faith in the Buddha as foremost,
Worthy of offerings, unsurpassed;

Having faith in the Dhamma as foremost,
The peace of detachment, bliss;
Having faith in the Sangha as foremost,
A field of merit, unsurpassed.

Distributing gifts among the foremost,
Foremost is the merit that accrues;
Foremost their life and beauty,
Fame, reputation, happiness and strength.

The wise one who gives to the foremost,
Concentrated on the foremost Dhamma,
Whether he becomes a deva or a human,
Rejoices in his foremost attainment.

91 A Means of Subsistence

This was said by the Lord . . . .

"Bhikkhus, this is a contemptible means of subsistence, this gathering of alms.[63] In the world, bhikkhus, it is a form of abuse to say, 'You alms-gatherer! Wandering about clutching a bowl!' Yet this means of subsistence has been taken up by young men of good family, for a reason, for a purpose. They have not been reduced to it by kings nor by robbers nor because of debt nor through fear nor from loss of an alternative means of livelihood, but with the thought: 'We are beset by birth, ageing and death, by sorrow, lamentation, pain, grief and despair; overcome by suffering, afflicted by suffering. Perhaps an end can be discerned of this whole mass of suffering.'

"So this young man of good family has gone forth (into homelessness), but he may be covetous for objects of desires, strongly passionate, malevolent-minded, corrupt in thought, unmindful, uncomprehending, unconcentrated, of wandering mind and uncontrolled faculties. Just as a brand from a funeral pyre, burned at both ends and in the middle smeared with excrement, can be used as timber neither in the village nor in the forest, so with such a comparison do I speak about this person: he has missed out on the enjoyments of a householder, yet he does not fulfil the purpose of recluseship."

He has missed both a layman's pleasure
And his recluseship, too, the luckless man!
Ruining it, he throws it away
And perishes like a funerary brand.

Far better for him to swallow
A fiery hot iron ball
Than that immoral and uncontrolled
He should eat the country's alms.[64]

92 The Hem of the Robe

This was said by the Lord . . . .

"Bhikkhus, even though a bhikkhu were to hold on to the hem of my robe and follow close behind me step by step, if he is covetous for objects of desire, strongly passionate, malevolent-minded, corrupt in thought, unmindful, uncomprehending, unconcentrated, of wandering mind and uncontrolled faculties, he is far from me and I from him. What is the reason? That bhikkhu does not see Dhamma. Not seeing Dhamma he does not see me.

"Bhikkhus, even though a bhikkhu should live a hundred leagues away, if he is not covetous for objects of desire, not strongly passionate, not malevolent-minded, uncorrupt in thought, with mindfulness established, clearly comprehending, concentrated, of unified mind and controlled faculties, he is close to me and I to him. What is the reason? That bhikkhu sees Dhamma. Seeing Dhamma, he sees me."

Though closely following behind,
Full of longings and resentment,
See how far away he is—
The desirous one from the desireless,
One unquenched from the quenched, [65]
A greedy one from the one without greed.

But a wise person who by direct knowledge
Has fully understood the Dhamma,
Becomes desireless and tranquil
Like a calm unruffled lake.

See how close he is to him—
A desireless one to the desireless,
One quenched to the quenched,
The greedless one to the one without greed.

93 The Fires

This was said by the Lord . . . .

"Bhikkhus, there are these three fires. What three? The fire of lust, the fire of hate, the fire of delusion. These, bhikkhus, are the three fires."

The fire of lust burns mortals [66]
Infatuated by sensual pleasures;
The fire of hate burns malevolent men
Who kill other living beings;

The fire of delusion burns the bewildered,
Ignorant of the Noble One's Dhamma.
Being unaware of these three fires,
Humankind delights in personal existence.[67]

Unfree from the bonds of Māra
They swell the ranks of hell,
Existence in the animal realm,
Asura-demons and the domain of ghosts.[68]

But those engaged in practising
The Enlightened One's teaching day and night
Ever perceiving the body's foulness,[69]
Extinguish the fire of lust.

Those best of men by loving-kindness
Extinguish the fire of hate,
And they extinguish the fire of delusion
By wisdom that leads to penetration.[70]

Having extinguished these fires,
Those discerning ones, unwearied
Night and day, attain final Nibbāna
And overcome all suffering.

The noble seers, masters of knowledge,
Wise ones with perfect understanding,
By directly knowing the end of birth
Come no more to renewal of being.

94 Investigating

This was said by the Lord . . . .

"Bhikkhus, a bhikkhu should so investigate that as he investigates, his consciousness is not distracted and diffused externally, and internally is not fixed, and so that by not grasping anything he remains undisturbed. If his consciousness is not distracted and diffused externally, and internally is not fixed, and if by not grasping anything he remains undisturbed, then there is no coming into existence of birth, ageing, death and suffering in the future."[71]

When a bhikkhu has abandoned
The seven ties and cut the cord,[72]
His wandering on in births is finished:
There is no renewal of being for him.

95 Sensual Desire

This was said by the Lord . . . .

"Bhikkhus, there are these three ways of obtaining the objects of sensual desire. What three? There are those objects of sensual desire already existent, there is the way of those who delight in creating them, and there is the way of those who gain control of objects created by others.[73] These are the three ways. . . ."

Those who enjoy what exists,
Those devas exercising control,
Those who delight in creating
And others who enjoy sense-objects —
Being in this state or another
They cannot pass beyond saṁsāra.[74]

Understanding this danger
In objects of sensual enjoyment,
Let the wise person abandon all sense pleasures,
Those both heavenly and human.[75]

By severing the flow of craving,
The flow so difficult to overcome
Of greed for pleasing, enticing forms,
They attain to final Nibbāna
And overcome all suffering.

The noble seers, masters of knowledge,
Wise ones with perfect understanding,
By directly knowing the end of birth
Come no more to renewal of being.

96 The Bonds

This was said by the Lord . . . .

"Bhikkhus, one bound by the bond of sensual desire and by the bond of being is a returner, one who comes back to this state. One freed from the bond of sensual desire but still bound by the bond of being is a non-returner, one who does not come back to this state. One freed from the bond of sensual desire and freed from the bond of being is an arahant, one in whom the taints are destroyed."[76]

Fettered by both these bonds —
The sensual bond and the bond of being —
Living beings continue in saṁsāra,
Journeying on to birth and death.

Those who abandon sensual desires
But have not reached the taints' destruction,
Fettered by the bondage of being,
Are declared to be non-returners.

But those who have cut off doubts,
Destroyed conceit and renewal of being,
Who reach the taints' full destruction,
Though in the world, have gone beyond.

97 Lovely Behaviour

This was said by the Lord . . . .

"Bhikkhus, a bhikkhu who is of lovely behaviour,

lovely nature and lovely wisdom is called in this Dhamma-and-discipline one who is fully accomplished, who has reached fulfilment, the supreme among men.

"And how is a bhikkhu of lovely behaviour? Here, bhikkhus, a bhikkhu is virtuous, he lives restrained by the restraint of the rules of discipline,[77] endowed with perfect conduct and resort; seeing danger in the slightest faults, he undertakes the rules of training and trains in them. In this way a bhikkhu is one who is of lovely behaviour. Thus he is of lovely behaviour.

"And how is he of lovely nature? Here, bhikkhus, a bhikkhu lives engaged in cultivating the seven groups of the requisites of enlightenment.[78] In this way a bhikkhu is one who is of lovely nature. Thus he is of lovely behaviour and lovely nature.

"And how is he of lovely wisdom? Here, bhikkhus, through realisation by his own direct knowledge, a bhikkhu here and now enters and abides in the mind-release and wisdom-release that are taintless by the destruction of the taints. In this way a bhikkhu is one who is of lovely wisdom.

"Thus he is of lovely behaviour, lovely nature and lovely wisdom. In this Dhamma-and-discipline he is called one who is fully accomplished, who has reached fulfilment and is supreme among men."

A conscientious bhikkhu
Who never does wrong in any way,
Not by body, speech or mind,
Is called "one of lovely behaviour."

An unassuming bhikkhu
Who has cultivated well the states
That lead to enlightenment
Is called "one of lovely nature."

A taintless bhikkhu
Who understands for himself
The end of suffering here
Is called "one of lovely wisdom."

He who excels in these three things,
Untroubled, with doubt destroyed,
Unattached in all the world,
Is called "one who has abandoned all." [79]

98 Giving

This was said by the Lord . . . .

"Bhikkhus, there are these two kinds of giving: the giving of material things and the giving of the Dhamma. Of these two kinds of giving, this is the foremost, namely, the giving of the Dhamma. There are these two kinds of sharing: the sharing of material things and the sharing of the Dhamma. Of these two kinds of sharing, this is the foremost, namely, the sharing of the Dhamma. There are these two kinds of help: help with material things and help with the Dhamma. Of these two kinds of help, this is the foremost, namely, help with the Dhamma."

When they say that giving
Is supreme and unsurpassed,
And the Lord himself has extolled sharing,
Who, wise and knowing,
Confident in that foremost field of merit,
Would not give at the appropriate time?

Both for those who proclaim it
And for those who listen to it, [80]
Confident in the Sublime One's teaching,
The supreme good is fully purified
As they live diligently in the teaching.

99 The Threefold Knowledge

This was said by the Lord . . . .

"Bhikkhus, I declare that it is through the Dhamma that one becomes a brahmin possessing the threefold knowledge; (I do not say this) of another merely because he can talk persuasively and recite.[81] And how do I declare that it is through the Dhamma that one becomes a brahmin possessing the threefold knowledge?

"Here, bhikkhus, a bhikkhu recollects a variety of former lives, that is, one birth, two births, three births, four births, five births, ten births, twenty births, thirty births, forty births, fifty births, a hundred births, a thousand births, a hundred thousand births; many aeons of world-contraction, many aeons of world-expansion, many aeons of both world-contraction and expansion. He recollects in a particular life being such a one by name, of such a clan, of such an appearance, having this kind of nutriment, experiencing these kinds of pleasure and pain, having this life-span; and deceasing from there he arose here. Thus with all their details and particulars he recollects a variety of former lives. This is the first knowledge attained by him. Ignorance is dispelled, knowledge arises; darkness is dispelled, light arises, as happens in one who lives diligent, ardent and resolute.

"Then again, bhikkhus, with the divine eye, which is purified and surpasses the human, a bhikkhu sees beings passing away and reappearing, inferior and superior, fair and ugly, fortunate and unfortunate, and he understands how beings pass on according to their deeds thus: 'Those worthy beings practising misconduct by body, speech and mind, insulters of the noble ones, of wrong view and undertaking deeds in consequence of wrong view, when the body perishes, have been reborn after death in a state of misery, a bad bourn, a state of ruin, hell. But those worthy beings practising good conduct by body, speech and mind, not insulters of the noble ones, of right view and undertaking deeds in consequence of right view, when the body perishes, have been reborn after death in a good bourn, a heavenly world.' Thus he sees this with the divine eye and he understands how beings pass on according to their deeds. This is the second knowledge attained by him. Ignorance is dispelled, knowledge arises; darkness is dispelled, light arises, as happens in one who lives diligent, ardent and resolute.

"Then again, bhikkhus, a bhikkhu, through realisation by his own direct knowledge, here and now enters and abides in the mind-release and wisdom-release that are taintless by the destruction of the taints. This is the third knowledge attained by him. Ignorance is dispelled, knowledge arises; darkness is dispelled, light arises, as happens in one who lives diligent, ardent and resolute."

"Thus, bhikkhus, do I declare that it is through the Dhamma that one becomes a brahmin possessing the threefold knowledge; (I do not say this) of another merely because he can talk persuasively and recite."

He who knows his former lives,
Who sees heaven and states of woe,
Who also reaches the end of birth,
A sage and master of direct knowledge —
By these three ways of knowing one becomes
A brahmin having the threefold knowledge.
That is what I call the threefold knowledge,
Not another's babbling and reciting.

This too is the meaning of what was said by the Lord, so I heard.

4

THE SECTION OF THE FOURS

100 The Dhamma-Offering

This was said by the Lord . . . .

"Bhikkhus, I am a brahmin, ever accessible to entreaties and open-handed,[1] one bearing his last body, an unsurpassed physician and surgeon.[2] You are my own legitimate sons, born from my mouth,[3] born of Dhamma, fashioned by Dhamma, heirs of Dhamma, not heirs of material things.

"Bhikkhus, there are these two kinds of giving: the giving of material things and the giving of the Dhamma. Of these two kinds of giving, this is the foremost, namely, the giving of the Dhamma. There are these two kinds of sharing . . . these two kinds of help . . . these two kinds of offerings:[4] the offering of material things and the offering of the Dhamma. Of these two kinds of offering, this is the foremost, namely, the offering of the Dhamma."

The Tathāgata who has made the Dhamma-offering,
Unselfish, compassionate towards all beings,
Living beings revere such a one,
Gone beyond being, as chief of devas and humans.

101 Easily Obtained

This was said by the Lord . . . .

"These four, bhikkhus, are trifling things, easily

obtained and blameless. What four? A robe made of cast-off rags is a trifling thing, easily obtained and blameless. Food gathered on almsround is a trifling thing, easily obtained and blameless. The root of a tree as a dwelling place is a trifling thing, easily obtained and blameless. Medicine consisting of putrid cow urine is a trifling thing, easily obtained and blameless.[5] These, bhikkhus, are the four trifling things, easily obtained and blameless. When a bhikkhu is content with these things that are trifling and easily obtained, I say of this person that he has the requisites for recluseship."

One content with what is blameless,
Things trifling and easily obtained,
Does not become vexed in mind
When not obtaining a place to live,
A robe to wear and food and drink;
He has no resentment in any quarter.

These are the things declared to be
Suitable for a recluse's life
By possession of which a bhikkhu
May abide content and diligent.

102 The Destruction of the Taints

This was said by the Lord . . . .

"For one knowing and seeing, bhikkhus, I say there is the destruction of the taints, not for one not knowing, not seeing. But for one knowing what, seeing what, is there the destruction of the taints? For one knowing and seeing, 'This is suffering,' there is the destruction of the taints. For one knowing and seeing, 'This is the origin of suffering' . . . 'This is the cessation of suffering' . . . 'This is the course leading to the cessation of suffering,' there is the destruction of the taints. Thus it is, bhikkhus, that for one knowing and seeing there is the destruction of the taints."

For a learner who is training
In conformity with the direct path,
The knowledge of destruction arises first,
And final knowledge immediately follows.[6]

To one freed by that final knowledge,
The topmost knowledge of freedom,
There arises the knowledge of destruction:
"Thus the fetters are destroyed."

Certainly not by the lazy person
Nor by the uncomprehending fool
Is Nibbāna to be attained,
The loosening of all worldly ties.

103 Recluses and Brahmins

This was said by the Lord . . . .

"Bhikkhus, whatever recluses and brahmins do not understand as it actually is: 'This is suffering'; 'This is the origin of suffering'; 'This is the cessation of suffering'; 'This is the course leading to the cessation of suffering'—these recluses and brahmins are not considered by me to be truly recluses among recluses, to be truly brahmins among brahmins. These venerable ones live without having realised and achieved here and now by their own direct knowledge the aim of being a recluse, the aim of being a brahmin.

"But, bhikkhus, whatever recluses and brahmins understand as it actually is: 'This is suffering'; 'This is the origin of suffering'; 'This is the cessation of suffering'; 'This is the course leading to the cessation of suffering'—these recluses and brahmins are considered by me to be truly recluses among recluses, to be truly brahmins among brahmins. These venerable ones indeed live having achieved and realised here and now by their own direct knowledge the aim of being a recluse, the aim of being a brahmin.'

Those who do not understand suffering,
Or how suffering is produced,
Or where suffering finally stops
Altogether without remainder,
And who do not know that path
Leading to relief from suffering—
They are destitute of mind-release
And lack release by wisdom too;
Unable to make an end of it,
They go on taking birth and ageing.

But those who understand suffering,
And how suffering is produced,
And where suffering finally stops
Altogether without remainder,
And who also know the path
Leading to relief from suffering—
They possess that mind-release
And the release by wisdom too;
Able to make an end of it
They never again take birth and age.

104 Excelling in Virtue

This was said by the Lord . . . .

"Bhikkhus, as to those bhikkhus who excel in virtue, excel in concentration, excel in wisdom, excel in release, excel in the knowledge and vision of release, who are advisors, instructors and demonstrators, who can exhort, inspire and encourage, and who are competent teachers of the true Dhamma—seeing those bhikkhus is very helpful, I say; listening to those bhikkhus, approaching them, attending upon them, remembering them, and following their example in going forth into homelessness is very helpful, I say. For what reason?

"By following such bhikkhus, by associating with them and attending upon them, the aggregate of virtue as yet incomplete reaches completion of development; the aggregate of concentration, of wisdom, of release and of knowledge and vision of release as yet incomplete reaches completion of development. Such bhikkhus as these are called teachers, caravan-leaders, fault-abandoners, dispellers of darkness, light-bringers, makers of radiance, luminaries, torch-bearers, bringers of illumination, noble ones, possessors of vision."

For those who are knowledgeable
This is a state making for joy—
Living the life of Dhamma
Under the noble ones perfected in mind.

They clarify the true Dhamma,
Shining forth and illuminating it,
Those light-bringers, heroic sages,
Endowed with vision, dispelling faults.

Having heard their teaching,
The wise with perfect understanding
By directly knowing the end of birth
Come no more to renewal of being.

105 Arousing Craving

This was said by the Lord . . . .

"Bhikkhus, there are four things that arouse craving whereby the craving that has arisen in a bhikkhu arises. What are the four? Because of robes, because of almsfood, because of a dwelling place, because of gaining this or losing that[7] the craving that has arisen in a bhikkhu arises. These, bhikkhus, are the four things that arouse craving whereby the craving that has arisen in a bhikkhu arises."

A man companioned by craving
Wanders on the long journey
In this state of being or another
And cannot go beyond saṁsāra.

Having understood the danger thus,
That craving is the origin of suffering,
A bhikkhu should wander mindfully,
Free from craving, without grasping.

106 With Brahmā

This was said by the Lord . . . .

"Living with Brahmā are those families where, within the home, mother and father are respected by the children.[8] Living with the early devas are those families where, within the home, mother and father are respected by the children. Living with the early teachers are those families where, within the home, mother and father are respected by the children.[9] Living with those worthy of adoration are those families where, within the home, mother and father are respected by the children. 'Brahmā,' bhikkhus, is a term for mother and father. 'Early devas' and 'early teachers' and 'those worthy of veneration' are terms for mother and father. For what reason? Because mother and father are very helpful to their children, they take care of them and bring them up and teach them about the world."

Mother and father are called
"Brahmā," "early teachers"
And "worthy of adoration,"
Being compassionate towards
Their family of children.

Thence the wise should venerate them,
Pay them due honour,
Provide them with food and drink,
Give them clothing and a bed,
Anoint and bathe them
And also wash their feet.

When he performs such service
For his mother and his father,
They praise that wise person even here
And hereafter he rejoices in heaven.

107 Very Helpful

This was said by the Lord . . . .

"Bhikkhus, brahmins and householders are very helpful to you. They provide you with the requisites of robes, almsfood, lodgings and medicine in time of sickness. And you, bhikkhus, are very helpful to brahmins and householders, as you teach them the Dhamma that is good at the outset, good in the middle and good at the end, with its correct meaning and wording, and you proclaim the holy life in its fulfilment and complete purity. Thus, bhikkhus, this holy life is lived with mutual support for the purpose of crossing the flood and making a complete end of suffering."

Householders and homeless alike,
Each a support for the other,
Both accomplish the true Dhamma —
The unsurpassed security from bondage.

From householders the homeless receive
These basic necessities of life,
Robes to wear and a place to dwell
Dispelling the hardships of the seasons.

And by relying on one of good conduct,[10]
Home-loving layfolk dwelling in a house
Place faith in those worthy ones[11]
Of noble wisdom and meditative.

Practising the Dhamma in this life,
The path leading to a good bourn,[12]
Those wishing for pleasure rejoice
In the delights of the deva world.

108 Deceitful

This was said by the Lord . . . .

"Bhikkhus, whatever bhikkhus are deceitful, stubborn, mere talkers, frauds, arrogant and unconcentrated, these bhikkhus are no followers of mine. They have turned aside from this Dhamma-and-discipline and will not achieve growth, progress or development within it.

"But whatever bhikkhus are not deceitful, not mere talkers, wise, adaptable and well concentrated, these bhikkhus are indeed my followers. They have not turned aside from this Dhamma-and-discipline and will achieve growth, progress and development within it."

Deceitful, stubborn, mere talkers,
Frauds, arrogant, unconcentrated —
These make no progress in the Dhamma
Taught by the Fully Enlightened One.

Undeceitful, not talkative, wise,
Adaptable, well concentrated —
Such as these progress in the Dhamma
Taught by the Fully Enlightened One.

109 The River Current

This was said by the Lord . . . .

"Suppose, bhikkhus, a man was being borne along by the current of a river that seemed pleasant and agreeable. But upon seeing him, a keen-sighted man standing on the bank would call out to him: 'Hey, good man! Although you are being borne along by the current of a river that seems pleasant and agreeable, lower down there is a pool with turbulent waves and swirling eddies, with monsters and demons.[13] On reaching that pool you will die or suffer close to death.' Then, bhikkhus, upon hearing the words of that person, that man would struggle against the current with hands and feet.

"I have made use of this simile, bhikkhus, to illustrate the meaning. And this is the meaning here: 'The current of the river' is a synonym for craving. 'Seeming pleasant and agreeable' is a synonym for the six internal sense-bases. 'The pool lower down' is a synonym for the five lower fetters.[14] 'Turbulent waves' is a synonym for anger and frustration. 'Swirling eddies' is a synonym for the five strands of sensual pleasure. 'Monsters and demons' is a synonym for womenfolk. 'Against the current' is a synonym for renunciation. 'Struggling with hands and feet' is a synonym for instigating energy. 'The keen-sighted man standing on the bank' is a synonym for the Tathāgata, the Arahant, the Fully Enlightened One."

Desiring future security from bondage
One should abandon sensual desire
However painful this is to do.[15]
Rightly comprehending with wisdom,
Possessing a mind that is well released,
One may reach freedom step by step.

One who is a master of knowledge,
Who has lived the holy life,
Is called one gone to the world's end,
One who has reached the further shore.

110 While Walking

This was said by the Lord . . . .

"Bhikkhus, if while walking a sensual thought or a thought of ill will or an aggressive thought arises in a bhikkhu, and if he tolerates it and does not reject it, does not dispel it and get rid of it and bring it to an end, that bhikkhu who in such a manner is lacking in ardour and unafraid of wrongdoing is called constantly lazy and indolent. If while standing . . . If while sitting . . . If while lying down a sensual thought or a thought of ill will or an aggressive thought arises in a bhikkhu, and if he tolerates it and does not reject it . . . that bhikkhu is called constantly lazy and indolent.

"But if while walking . . . standing . . . sitting . . . lying down a sensual thought or a thought of ill will or an aggressive thought arises in a bhikkhu and he does not tolerate it, but rejects it, dispels it, gets rid of it and brings it to an end, that bhikkhu who in such a manner is ardent and afraid of wrongdoing is called constantly energetic and resolute."

Whether walking or standing,
Sitting or lying down

Whoever thinks such thoughts
That are evil and worldly—
He is following a wrong path,
Infatuated with delusive things.
Such a bhikkhu cannot reach
Enlightenment which is supreme.

Whether walking or standing,
Sitting or lying down,
Whoever overcomes these thoughts,
Delighting in the quelling of thoughts —
Such a bhikkhu is able to reach
Enlightenment which is supreme.

111 Perfect in Virtue

This was said by the Lord . . . .

"Bhikkhus, you should live perfect in virtue, perfect in the practice of the rules of discipline and be restrained by the restraint of the rules. Perfect in conduct and resort, seeing danger in the slightest faults, you should train in the rules of training you have undertaken. Living perfect in virtue, bhikkhus, . . . and training in the rules of training you have undertaken, what is there further that should be done?

"If while he is walking, standing, sitting and lying down a bhikkhu is free from covetousness and ill will, free from sloth and torpor, free from restlessness and worry, and has abandoned doubts, his energy becomes strong and unflagging, his mindfulness is alert and unclouded, his body is calm and undistressed, his mind concentrated and one-pointed. A bhikkhu who in such a manner is ardent and afraid of wrongdoing is called constantly energetic and resolute."

Controlled while walking,
Controlled while standing,
Controlled while sitting,
Controlled while reclining,
Controlled in bending and
Stretching his limbs —
Above, across and below,
As far as the world extends,
A bhikkhu observes how things occur,
The arising and passing of the aggregates.

Living thus ardently,
Of calm and quiet conduct,
Ever mindful, he trains in the course
Of calm tranquility of mind.
Such a bhikkhu is said to be
One who is ever resolute.

112 The World

This was said by the Lord, said by the Arahant, so I heard:

"Bhikkhus, the world has been fully understood by the Tathāgata; the Tathāgata is released from the world.[16] The origin of the world has been fully understood by the Tathāgata; the origin of the world has been abandoned by the Tathāgata. The cessation of the world has been fully understood by the Tathāgata; the cessation of the world has been realised by the Tathāgata. The course leading to the cessation of the world has been fully understood by the Tathāgata; the course leading to the cessation of the world has been developed by the Tathāgata.

"Bhikkhus, in the world with its devas, māras and brahmās, with its recluses and brahmins, among humankind with its princes and people, whatever is seen, heard, sensed, cognised, attained, sought and reflected upon by the mind—that is fully understood by the Tathāgata: therefore he is called the Tathāgata.

"Bhikkhus, from the night when the Tathāgata awakened to unsurpassed full enlightenment until the night when he passes away into the Nibbāna-element with no residue left, whatever he speaks, utters and explains—all that is just so and not otherwise: therefore he is called the Tathāgata.

"As the Tathāgata says, so he does; as the Tathāgata does, so he says: therefore he is called the Tathāgata.

"In the world with its devas, māras and brahmās, with its recluses and brahmins, among humankind with its princes and people, the Tathāgata is the conqueror, unvanquished, all-seer, wielding power: therefore he is called the Tathāgata."

By knowledge of the whole world,
The whole world as it truly is,
He is released from all the world,
In all the world he is unattached.

The all-conquering heroic sage,
Freed from every bond is he;
He has reached that perfect peace,
Nibbāna which is free from fear.

Rid of taints, he is enlightened,
Trouble-free, with doubts destroyed,
Reached the final end of deeds,[17]
Released by clinging's full destruction.

The Enlightened One, the Lord,
A lion is he, unsurpassed;
For in the world together with its devas
He set the Brahma-wheel in motion.[18]

Thus those devas and human beings,
Gone for refuge to the Buddha,
On meeting him pay homage to him,
The great one free from diffidence.

Tamed, of the tamed he is the best;
Calmed, of the calmed he is the seer;
Freed, of the freed he is the foremost;
Crossed, of the crossed he is the chief.

Thus do they pay him due homage,
The great one free from diffidence:
"In the world together with its devas
There is no person equalling you."

This too is the meaning of what was said by the Lord, so I heard.

NOTES

The Section of The Ones

1. These introductory and concluding words found in each sutta are omitted after this first discourse to avoid unnecessary repetition. *Attha*: both the meaning (significance and intention) of the Buddha's words, and the aim or goal of the Teaching.

2. Non-returning (*anāgāmitā*) is the third stage of the noble path, above stream-entry and once-returning but below arahantship. One who has reached this stage eradicates the fetters of sensual desire and ill will and is reborn in one of the five celestial realms called the Pure Abodes (*suddhāvāsa*), there to attain arahantship. Comy. points out that greed (*lobha*) is used here, not as a comprehensive equivalent of craving, but specifically to mean sensual lust (*kāmarāga*). While the non-returner abandons sensual lust, greed for being is eliminated only by the arahant.

3. This refers to the three subhuman realms of existence: hell, the animal realm and the world of hungry ghosts (*peta*).

4. In contrast to greed, hate (*dosa*) is eliminated in its entirety by the path of the non-returner. According to the Comy., among the unwholesome qualities mentioned in the following suttas, it should be understood that anger and contempt are fully eradicated by the non-returner, while delusion and conceit are eliminated only in part, their full eradication requiring attainment of the path of arahantship.

5. According to the Comy., the "All" refers to *sakkāya-dhammā*: the factors of personality, that is, the five aggregates of grasping (*upādānakkhandha*)—form, feeling, perception, mental activities and consciousness. These comprise the "all" or totality of our experience. Comy. explains "direct knowledge" (*abhiññā*) as knowing things in a superior mode by way of their undistorted characteristics. "Full understanding" (*pariññā*) is explained as the investigation of conditioned things as impermanent, suffering and not self, culminating in the abandonment of attachment.

6. Or repeated birth, *punabbhava*. See Ud. 3.10. *Bhava*: being, becoming or existence, is one of the factors in the formula of dependent arising (*paṭicca samuppāda*). Being arises from grasping and leads to birth, death and suffering.

7. These five discourses have been abbreviated as they merely repeat the previous one, substituting greed, etc., for conceit. The verses are identical with those of 1-5.

8. Ignorance (*avijjā*)—synonymous with delusion (*moha*)—about suffering, its origin in craving, its cessation and the noble eightfold path that leads to its cessation. Saṁsāra is the perpetual wandering on from birth to birth, the cycle of rebirths.

9. *Anga* means a limb or constituent part, hence, as here and in the next discourse, an essential factor or requirement for gaining release. Wise attention (*yoniso manasikāra*) means attending to aspects of a thing or situation in a way that is helpful in the practice of the path. The commentaries mention considering things as impermanent, unsatisfactory, without self, and foul rather than the opposites, and the avoidance of fruitless speculation.

10. A learner (*sekha*) is a noble disciple who has not yet become an arahant, but is training himself for that goal. The arahant or perfected one is called an *asekha:* one who has no more to learn, who has completed the training. Supreme security from bondage, *anuttara yogakkhema,* is release from the four bonds (*yogā*): sensual desire, desire for being, views and ignorance.

11. In Vism. Chap. III the good friend (*kalyāṇamitta*) is a teacher, the giver of the meditation subject, and in S. 3:18/i, 88 it is said that good friendship encourages one to develop and cultivate the noble eightfold path. In this same discourse the Buddha says: "It is because of my being a good friend, Ānanda, that beings liable to birth are released from birth, that beings liable to old age are released from old age, that beings liable to sickness . . . death . . . sorrow . . . suffering . . . despair are released from despair."

12. The fetters (*saṁyojana*) are ten in number: personality view, doubt, clinging to external observances, sensual lust, ill will, craving for form, craving for the formless, conceit, restlessness and ignorance. The stream-enterer has cut off the first three; the once-returner has also weakened the fourth and fifth; the non-returner has removed the first five; and the arahant has destroyed all ten.

13. The Comy. refers to the schism in the Sangha created by Devadatta, the Buddha's cousin. Concerning Devadatta see Sutta 89 and notes. Maliciously creating a schism in the Sangha leads to immediate rebirth in hell for an aeon.

14. Those ordinary people whose faith is as yet undeveloped (Comy.), that is, those people who, without committing themselves, have shown an interest in the Buddha's teaching.

15. A *kappa,* an aeon or world-cycle, is in Buddhist cosmology a vast period of time during which the universe evolves and declines, expands and contracts. These periodic cycles continue without beginning or end.

16. "(He) is not deprived": he is not excluded from attaining security or freedom from the four bonds and thus becoming an arahant. See note 10 above.

17. This is a difficult idiomatic phrase that occurs in several places in the Pali Canon. Comy. explains: "Just as something that has been carried is cast aside, so he is placed in hell, having been conveyed there by his own (bad) deeds." That this is intended is made clearer in the third verse.

18. Netti, pp. 130–31, has a somewhat different version of this (and the next) discourse, both in the prose and the verse. See *The Guide*, pp. 177–78. The Netti adds some extra lines of verse and in the first stanza replaces "the Buddha" by "the Teacher" (*satthā*), the more usual epithet in such contexts.

19. *Pasannacitta:* a clear, bright, purified and confident mind. According to the Comy., it means having faith in the Three Jewels and in actions (*kamma*) and their results.

20. He knows from personal experience by remembering his former lives.

21. Loving-kindness (*mettā*) is the first of the four "divine abidings" (*brahmavihāra*) or boundless states, the other three being compassion, sympathetic joy and equanimity.

22. The plane of Streaming Radiance (*ābhassara*) is not included in the destruction at the end of the aeon. When a new universe begins, beings come from there

to inhabit it, the first to be born being the Great Brahmā, a high divinity in the Buddhist cosmos.

23. Sakka is the chief god or deva of the Tāvatiṁsa (the heaven of the "Thirty-three"), one of the heavens of the sensuous world (*kāma-loka*), which is below the form world (*rūpa-loka*) inhabited by the brahmās.

24. The *cakkavattī-rājā* or righteous Wheel-turning Monarch is the worldly equivalent of the Buddha. It was prophesied of the Bodhisatta, the Buddha-to-be, that if he remained a householder, he would become a Wheel-turning Monarch, but if he went forth into homelessness, he would become a Fully Enlightened One and turn the "Wheel of Dhamma" instead of the "Wheel of Conquest." The seven jewels are emblems of royalty: the wheel-jewel, the elephant-jewel, the horse-jewel, the woman-jewel, the gem-jewel, the steward-jewel and the counselor-jewel. See M. 129.

25. *Dāna,* giving or generosity, is traditionally the most basic source of "merit" in all Buddhist lands. Self-mastery (*dama*) is control of the mind and the senses so that passion, etc. do not overwhelm one. Refraining (*saññama*) is control of bodily actions and speech. Thus these three cover all possible ways of performing voluntary actions.

26. Diligence (*appamāda*) means being energetic and ever mindful in cultivating what is good and wholesome; it is the foundation of all progress. Its opposite is negligence (*pamāda*) by which the mind is distracted from the good and becomes overwhelmed by defilements.

27. This refers to the stream-enterer, who is reborn at most seven times more before attaining release.

28. "If they were to enjoy, as I now enjoy" (Comy.).

29. *Bhuñjati* means both to eat and to enjoy, to make use of something.

30. The "three grounds for making merit" (*puññakiriyavatthu*) are giving, virtue and mind-development. See Sutta 60. Comy. glosses "productive of a future birth" (*opadhikāni*) as meaning productive of a successful individual existence, yielding results at conception and during life. The term is contrasted with grounds for making merit aimed at release from future birth, such as by developing insight.

31. Mind-release (*cetovimutti*) is the culmination of the mind's purgation of emotional impurities by the practice of tranquility (*samatha*). There are various kinds of mind-release, and although they are very exalted, the only one that is irreversible is the unshakable mind-release (*akuppā cetovimutti*) possessed by an arahant. The practice of loving-kindness, the first of the four divine abidings, culminates in the boundless mind-release (*appamāṇā cetovimutti*) in which all ill will or malice (*vyāpāda*) is removed from the mind.

32. It is by being practised towards all beings equally and without exception, not just towards one person, that loving-kindness becomes boundless and the basis for mind-release.

33. This refers to the legendary kings of the past who ruled righteously and made sacrifices to the gods and gave abundant alms to the needy after their victories. Later they abdicated to become seers (*isi*), hermits or holy men, and then went to heaven. The sacrifices are mentioned in the Sutta Nipāta (v. 303) as having been initiated by corrupt brahmins desirous of accumulating wealth. *Soma* is the sacrificial drink offered in libations to the gods.

THE SECTION OF THE TWOS

1. The senses are regarded as "doors" by which sense objects as well as unwholesome states enter the mind. They are guarded by mindfulness. Being immoderate in eating (literally, "not knowing the measure in food") is eating without wisely reflecting and for purposes other than merely the upkeep of the body and physical health.

2. *Akatabhīruttāna*. Comy. explains: "he has not done what gives protection to oneself from danger." Hence this phrase has been rendered "(not done) what is beneficial."

3. "Bad behaviour" (*pāpaka sīla*) refers to immoral conduct, uncontrolled behaviour that is considered wrong (Comy.). The word *sīla* does not mean only moral conduct and precepts, but also behaviour generally. "Bad view" is of various kinds, such as the view that actions (*kamma*) do not produce results (*vipāka*).

4. The restraint of wrong behaviour by moral conduct and of unwholesome states of mind by mindfulness, and the abandoning of the defilements by meditation and wisdom.

5. *Anītiha:* not handed down by tradition or based upon hearsay as is the Vedic lore of the brahmins. The Buddha teaches from his own direct experience of enlightenment.

6. Direct knowledge (*abhiññā*) includes various kinds of supernormal powers, such as the recollection of past lives, and also the knowledge of the destruction of the taints (*āsavā*), which is the attainment of arahantship. Full understanding (*pariññā*) is penetrative insight into phenomena and their characteristics as impermanent, unsatisfactory and not self. Here, according to the

Comy., the two terms mean knowledge and penetration of the four noble truths.

7. This verse is identical with that in Sutta 35 above.

8. That is, he has a reason for beginning to exert himself.

9. He is moved by a sense of urgency (*saṁvega*) on seeing the suffering inherent in the saṁsāric round of birth, old age and death, and he makes a proper endeavour (*yoniso padhāna*), wise or skilful endeavour or right effort, to attain release.

10. *Tathāgata* is a term often used by the Buddha when referring to himself. Briefly it means "He who has thus come" or "thus gone" (to enlightenment). The commentaries give a long and detailed explanation. For a translation, see Bhikkhu Bodhi, *The Discourse on the All-Embracing Net of Views* (BPS, 1978), pp. 331 ff. See also Sutta 112 below.

11. Comy.: The thought of security (*khemavitakka*) is especially connected with compassion (*karuṇā*), though it also occurs connected with loving-kindness and sympathetic joy. It is the forerunner and concomitant of the Buddha's attainment of great compassion as well as of his attainment of loving-kindness, etc. The thought of solitude (*pavivekavitakka*) is the forerunner and concomitant of his attainment of fruition, though it also occurs in connection with the jhānas, etc.

12. Non-ill will (*avyāpajjha*) is a synonym for loving-kindness (*mettā*).

13. Or "movable or immovable" (*tasaṁ vā thāvaraṁ vā*). According to the Comy. it means those with craving and those without craving (i.e. arahants). This is the first thought, the thought of security, indicative of the Buddha's great compassion.

14. Comy. identifies solitude here with the eradication and subsiding of defilements that occurred with the Buddha's attainment of enlightenment, and also with the ultimate solitude of Nibbāna, the escape from all conditioned things.

15. Comy.: He endured or carried the entire equipment for supreme enlightenment and the undertaking of great compassion, which no one other than a great Bodhisatta could endure or carry; and he conquered Māra, whom no one else could conquer; and he performed the tasks of a Buddha, which no one else could perform.

16. *Vissantara* (PTS ed.), *vessantara* (Sinh. ed.), *visantara* (Bms. ed.). Comy. explains etymologically: "He is called thus because he has expelled unrighteousness (*visamassa vantattā*) such as unrighteous bodily conduct, etc.; or because he guides others across after he himself has crossed over (*taritvā*) the poison (*visa*) of all defilements, or the poison of all the suffering of the round."

17. Māra is the Evil One, the personification of all that prevents our attainment of enlightenment. The Commentaries explain Māra as the defilements, the five aggregates and death, also as the Tempter, an evil deity.

18. This verse also occurs at M. 26 (i.168).

19. On shame and fear of wrongdoing, see Sutta 42 and note 22.

20. Clinging to name and form (*nāmarūpa*), or the five aggregates, ordinary people (mis-) conceive them as being a self or as belonging to self.

21. Penetration of the four noble truths.

22. *Sukka* means bright, pure, good, and refers to those qualities that are virtuous and wholesome, by

which the mind is cleansed and purified and made radiant. "Shame" (*hiri*) is the inwardly arisen disgust with evil, the voice of conscience which inhibits one from doing wrong; "fear of wrongdoing" (*ottappa*) is the outwardly directed fear of the painful consequences of evil and fear of being blamed by others. The two are said to be the foundation of morality.

23. The prose portion to follow is identical with the inspired utterance in Ud. 8.3. This discourse contrasts the unconditioned, Nibbāna, with what is caused and conditioned. The verses continue the contrast by listing synonyms for each of the two terms, concluding with the appropriate evaluation of each.

24. Nutriment is fourfold: material food, contact, mental volition and consciousness. All are essential to support life. Thus, according to the Buddha, "mental food" is as important for the mind as material food is for the upkeep of the body. "Craving's cord" (*netti*) is craving for being—see note 29 below.

25. The taints (*āsava*) are sensual desire, desire for being, and ignorance. See Sutta 56. "One in whom the taints are destroyed" (*khīṇāsava*) is another name for an arahant.

26. The attainment of arahantship consists in the extinction of the defilements (*kilesa-parinibbāna*)—attachment, hate and delusion—and while the arahant continues to live out his life, his freedom from defilements is called "the Nibbāna-element with residue left" (*sa-upādisesa-nibbānadhātu*). The "residue" is the five aggregates—the mind and the body and the senses—that continue to function.

27. As there is no craving and clinging ("delight"), at the arahant's death, when the body perishes there is nothing to be projected into a future birth. Thus there

takes place the final extinction of the aggregates (*khandha-parinibbāna*), which is "the Nibbāna-element with no residue left" (*anupādisesa-nibbānadhātu*).

28. *Tādi*: "serene," is a term for an emancipated one, the arahant, and refers to his equanimity towards agreeable and disagreeable sense objects.

29. The "cord of being" (*bhavanetti*) is craving for being (*bhavataṇhā*), so called because it keeps living beings attached to the round of existence.

30. *Paṭisallāna.* Comy. explains as physical solitude (*kāyaviveka*), the prerequisite for mental seclusion achieved by meditation.

31. Comy. glosses insight (*vipassanā*) as the sevenfold contemplation: of impermanence, suffering, not self, dispassion, detachment, cessation and relinquishment.

32. Comy.: The five aggregates as impermanent, etc.

33. Māra, the Evil One, is conceived as leading a large army (of defilements) which must be faced and defeated to gain enlightenment.

34. This refers to the cultivation of insight and understanding after establishing mindfulness, clarity and calm tranquility of mind as a basis. Comy. also mentions the cultivation of the *bojjhangas*, the seven factors of enlightenment: mindfulness, investigation, energy, rapture, tranquility, concentration and equanimity.

35. These verses are found at Dhp. 306-308.

36. The cessation of being (*bhavanirodha*) is Nibbāna.

37. Those who strongly crave for being and delight in it incline towards the eternalist view which posits a self existing eternally in some form after death. Thus they "hold back" from Nibbāna as the cessation of being.

38. Those who crave for non-being or personal annihil-

ation "overreach" in adopting an annihilationist view. Both the eternalist and the annihilationist fall into the trap of thinking in static terms about the "self," i.e. that there is a permanent self which continues forever (eternalism) or else is permanent only for a fixed period during life and stops at death (annihilationism).

39. The correct attitude of "those with vision," according to the Buddha, is to avoid thinking in terms of "self" and to tackle the root of the problem by eradicating the ignorance and craving that give rise to both wrong views.

The Section of The Threes

1. *Tacasāraṁ.* Comy. explains that this is a name for the bamboo, so called because its pith is exposed outside rather than concealed within. These plants die after seeding.

2. The form element (*rūpadhātu*) is the realm of subtle form, the worlds of the brahmās and the jhānas that lead to rebirth into that realm. The formless element (*arūpadhātu*) is the formless realm and the formless jhānas that lead to rebirth there. The element of cessation (*nirodhadhātu*) is Nibbāna.

3. The point is not to settle in "form" or in the "formless," which are blissful and peaceful states attained through meditation, but to realise that they are still subject to impermanence and death. Only in Nibbāna is perfect freedom to be found. The attainment of jhānic absorption can be such a profound experience that it may easily be mistaken for the ultimate goal. In fact, entire religions and theologies have been founded upon and reinforced by such experiences.

4. *Kāyena phassayitvā.* Literally, "having touched with the body." According to the Comy., "body" (*kāya*) in

this context denotes the mind or mental factors (*nāma-kāya*) rather than the physical body (*rūpakāya*).

5. By penetrative understanding of feelings according to the method of the four noble truths and by attaining the noble path of the arahant. Feelings are seen as the truth of suffering, as is shown in the next sutta (No. 53). They originate in contact (*phassa*) and lead to craving, as stated in the formula of dependent arising (*paṭicca samuppāda*).

6. Because it is unstable and liable to change.

7. Search (*esanā*) is a questing or seeking and a form of longing that arises through ignorance and craving.

8. According to the Comy., "the search for a holy life" means seeking and holding various wrong views such as eternalism and annihilationism, various theories about the soul and the world, etc. (see Ud. 6.4 - 6.6).

9. Māra is depicted leading his army into battle while mounted upon an elephant.

10. Māra's domain is the whole of conditioned existence over which he exercises control.

11. A non-learner (*asekha*) is an arahant, one who has no more to learn, who has completed the course of training.

12. Virtue, concentration and wisdom that are complete and perfected. These three are called the three trainings (*sikkhā*) and form the threefold division of the noble eightfold path.

13. These verses are identical to those in Sutta 22 above.

14. The fleshly eye (*maṁsa-cakkhu*) is the physical sense-organ, the vision of which is limited in comparison to the other two. The divine or heavenly eye (*dibba-*

cakkhu) is one of the direct knowledges (*abhiññā*) by which one sees the arising and passing away of beings according to their deeds. The wisdom eye (*paññā-cakkhu*) is that which penetrates the four noble truths.

15. Comy. states that the occurrence of the fleshly eye is the path, or basis, for the divine eye; for the divine eye arises in one whose natural sight is unimpaired, since he arouses the divine eye by extending the light of the *kasiṇa* object, and he cannot do so without having first acquired the learning sign (*uggahanimitta*) in the *kasiṇa* disk.

16. Comy.: The knowledge of the destruction of the taints arises from the wisdom eye. By arousing and developing the eye of noble wisdom, one is released from all the suffering of the round (of existence).

17. They are faculties (*indriya*) in the sense of ruling, controlling and dominating other factors associated with themselves. There are altogether twenty-two faculties arranged under various groupings of which the three listed here are the exclusively supramundane faculties.

18. Comy.: The first is the wisdom pertaining to the path of stream-entry. It is so called because it arises to one who had, prior to the attainment of the path, practised with the determination, "I shall know what I have never known before in this beginningless saṁsāra—the deathless state (i.e. Nibbāna), or the four noble truths." The second is the faculty of wisdom in the six supramundane states from the fruition of stream-entry through the path of arahantship. And the third is the consummate knowledge of the four noble truths which arises in the arahant with the attainment of the final fruition.

19. *Ujumagga*: the noble path leading directly to Nibbāna.

20. Comy. gives two interpretations of this couplet: (1) first arises the knowledge of the path of arahantship, called "destruction" because it destroys all defilements; and immediately after there arises arahantship itself, here called "final knowledge" (*aññā*); (2) first there arises the knowledge of the path of stream-entry, called "destruction" because it destroys the defilements coexisting with wrong views; and immediately afterwards there arises the faculty of final knowledge, which persists through the path of arahantship.

21. The arahant, endowed with the third faculty, delights in the peaceful state (*santipada*), which is Nibbāna.

22. According to the Comy., beings identify one or the other of the five aggregates as the "self," and from that standpoint they proceed to speculate with regard to the three times: "Was I in the past? . . . Having been what, what did I become in the past? . . . What will I become in the future?" And in the present they think: "Where has this being come from, where will it go?" (M. 2, etc.). The concept of a "self," of an "I," is the basic fallacy.

23. He does not misconceive or imagine that there is a permanent self that speaks, acts and exists in the three times. Through full understanding (*pariññā*) he has realised phenomena to be impermanent, suffering and not self.

24. He takes his stand on Dhamma, on Nibbāna (the state of peace), which is timeless (*akāliko*) and stands outside the three periods of time.

25. Comy.: The arahant does not come to renewed being in any state of existence, and thus he no more

enters into the range of concepts specifying his personal identity. He goes to the indescribable state, the unconditioned Nibbāna.

26. These verses and those of the following sutta appeared in Suttas 30 and 31 above.

27. There is a play on words here which is lost in translation: *moneyya*, translated as "perfection," is the state of a *muni*, a sage, a perfect or silent one, one who has *mona*: wisdom, self-possession, silence (the silencing of all imperfections). Thus *moneyya* is the silencing or stilling of activities (*kamma*) of body, speech and mind, imperfections that lead to a future birth.

28. By the development of virtue, concentration and wisdom.

29. "Supreme" here is *brahma*, which Comy. explains as the best (*seṭṭha*), i.e. the fruit of arahantship. Comy. also explains "Tathāgata," usually an exclusive epithet of the Buddha, in a way applicable to all arahants: like other arahants, so (*tathā*) this noble person has come along (*āgata*) endowed with excellent supporting conditions from the past and has gone (*gata*) to Nibbāna along the Middle Way.

30. The symbolic meaning of these terms is explained in Sutta 109. In the case of bhikkhunīs (Buddhist nuns) "womenfolk" should be replaced by "menfolk." M. 67 offers a partly different interpretation of the metaphor.

31. This statement is an idiomatic phrase and is apparently a quotation from an unknown source, describing one who has attained his goal. It is found elsewhere, e.g. at S. 35:197/iv. 175, as a designation for an arahant. See *Saṁyutta Nikāya Anthology* I (BPS, Wheel No. 107/109), p. 67.

32. The King of Death (*maccurāja*) is a name for Māra.

The arahant, by not being reborn, vanishes from Māra's sight, he steps outside Māra's domain so that the "Evil One" can neither locate nor define (delimit, measure, *pamāṇa*) him.

33. The terms "recluse" and "brahmin" often occur together and denote those leading a life involved with religion. A recluse (*samaṇa*) is defined as anyone who has gone forth from the house life and in the Indian context could be called "a holy man." A brahmin is a priest who performs rituals and sacrifices and is usually a householder. The Buddha is sometimes called the "Great Recluse" (*mahāsamaṇa*).

34. Renunciation (*nekkhamma*) refers here to the first absorption (*jhāna*), which is the entry into the form-realm (*rūpāvacara*) by leaving behind the realm of sensual desires (*kāmāvacara*); it is attained when the mind is "isolated" (*vivicca*) from sensual desires and other unwholesome states. The "formless" (*āruppa*) is a formless-sphere meditative attainment. "Cessation" (*nirodha*) is Nibbāna.

35. *Sabbasankhārasamatha*: the cessation of all conditioned things, of the whole of conditioned existence; this is Nibbāna, the unconditioned state.

36. The second verse appears also in Sutta 53.

37. The second and third verses are identical with those in Sutta 51, except for a slight variation in the first line of the second verse.

38. These are the five precepts which, together with the three refuges, are the basic rules of conduct and belief for all Buddhists.

39. He himself gives and enjoins others to do likewise.

40. *Tagara:* a sweet-scented powder obtained from the tagara shrub.

41. "Element" (*dhātu*) here means disposition or temperament *(ajjhāsaya)*.

42. *Kamma*: here, various kinds of work, such as robe-making and so forth.

43. *Anavaññatti*: wanting to be well regarded by others, a form of arrogance or pride.

44. *Parānuddayatā*. Ordinarily, this might mean having sympathy or compassion for others, but in this context it means an unwholesome state, a love of socialising and an emotional involvement with others leading to loss of independence.

45. *Bodhipakkhiyadhammā.* The seven groups are: the four foundations of mindfulness; the four right efforts; the four bases of successful accomplishment; the five faculties; the five powers; the seven factors of enlightenment (see The Twos, note 34) and the noble eightfold path. See Ledi Sayadaw, *The Requisites of Enlightenment* (BPS, Wheel No. 171/174, 1971).

46. Wisdom-release (*paññāvimutti*) is the knowledge associated with the fruition-attainment of the arahant (*arahattaphala*). Mind-release (*cetovimutti*) is the arahant's freedom from the negative emotions of greed, hate and delusion. See also Sutta 27 and the accompanying note concerning mind-release.

47. Reading here *tanhi tassa na passanti yena maccuvasaṁ vaje*. The PTS edition is surely mistaken in reading, in the third line, *namassanti* instead of *na passanti*.

48. By reason of the attainment of the noble path (*ariyamagga*).

49. *Opadhikam*. As a foundation or basis for future births.

50. Contemplating foulness (*asubha*) is reflecting on the body in various ways so as to overcome physical attachment and sensual lust. The most common method is by mentally dissecting the body into its (traditional) thirty-two parts: head hair, body hair, nails, teeth, skin, etc. The practice of the cemetery contemplations is also used. See Vism., Chapters VI and VIII.

51. The practice of *ānāpānasati*, or mindfulness of in-and-out breathing, is the most effective way of controlling the wandering thoughts that prevent the attainment of tranquility and concentration.

52. The practice of speaking and thinking what is not according to Dhamma.

53. Or non-ill will (*avyāpāda*). In Pali, unlike English, negative words are actual synonyms of their positive counterparts. Thus "non-blindness" is a synonym for sight, "non-ill will" for friendliness or loving-kindness (*mettā*), "harmlessness" for compassion, etc. This makes it difficult to find exact equivalents for all these terms.

54. These three are called the three unwholesome roots (*akusala-mūlāni*) in Sutta 50.

55. Devadatta was the Buddha's cousin who attempted to usurp the Buddha's position as leader of the Sangha. According to the Comy., because of pride in his attainments, Devadatta reasoned thus: "The Buddha is a Sakyan, I also am a Sakyan; the Buddha is a recluse, I am also a recluse; the Buddha possesses supernormal powers (*iddhi*), I also possess supernormal powers; . . . I will be a Buddha and take care of the Order of bhikkhus." When this bid failed he attempted to create a schism within the Sangha and plotted to have the Buddha murdered. See Bhikkhu Ñāṇamoli, *The Life of the Buddha*, pp. 258ff.

56. The "trifling attainment" refers to Devadatta's acquisition of various supernormal powers, which led to his downfall.

57. The first line of this verse is translated following the Burmese-script edition, *samānam anuciṇṇo,* in preference to the PTS reading, *pamādam anuciṇṇo.*

58. The Unremitting Hell *(avīci-niraya)* is the lowest and most painful of the several Buddhist hells (both hot and cold).

59. *Aggappasāda*: foremost (highest, best) faith, confidence, devotion.

60. Enabling one to enter the noble path (*ariyamagga*) and so gain release.

61. "States": *dhammā,* all phenomena that exist, Nibbāna alone being the unconditioned (*asankhata*) state.

62. Each of the four kinds of noble disciple is considered as either being on the path (*magga*) or as having attained the fruit (*phala*) of that path; thus there are four pairs or eight individuals.

63. *Piṇḍolya* (lit., food-balls or lumps) means the almsfood a bhikkhu collects from house to house.

64. This verse appears also in Sutta 48. The Burmese-script edition includes here also the preceding verse of Sutta 48, though the PTS edition, which I follow, excludes it.

65. *Nibbuto*: quenched or cooled. One who has extinguished the three fires of lust, hate and delusion (see Sutta 93) has attained Nibbāna, the state of extinction or being "quenched."

66. *Macce*: those subject to death (*maccu*) and rebirth; or those under the sway of Māra, the Evil One, of *maccurāja*, the King of Death.

67. *Sakkāya*: the group of factors constituting individual existence, conceived by the ignorant to be permanent, pleasurable and the "self." It is identified as the five aggregates of grasping (*upādānakkhandhā*).

68. These are the four bad bourns. The *asuras*—an addition to the usual set of three bad bourns—are a type of titan or demon obsessed by the urge for power.

69. See above, note 50.

70. Penetration (*nibbedha*) is the direct understanding of the four noble truths. See the verse in Sutta 41.

71. In the Uddesavibhanga Sutta (M. 138) this highly compressed statement by the Buddha is explained by the venerable Mahākaccāna and forms the subject matter of that sutta. Briefly, "externally not distracted" means guarding the senses so that the mind is not overwhelmed and carried away by the variety and details of sights, sounds, etc., that impinge on the senses. "Internally not fixed" is not being fascinated by the rapture and joy, etc., experienced in the jhānas. Such fascination is a subtle form of craving which leads to grasping, being, birth and so forth, that is, to the whole process of future suffering and the perpetuation of saṁsāra. Investigating (examining, probing) these experiences is the practice of insight meditation (*vipassanā-bhāvanā*).

72. The seven ties (*sangā*) are: craving, views, conceit, anger, ignorance, defilement and misconduct. The "cord" is the cord of being (*bhavanetti*), i.e. craving for being. See The Twos, note 29.

73. Humans and most devas are surrounded by objects that can become objects of desire—this is the first way. The second and third refer to two classes of devas in the world of sense (*kāmadhātu*): the *nimmānarati*-

devas ("those delighting in their own creations") and the *parinimmita-vasavatti-devas* ("those who control what others have created"). The verse also mentions "others who enjoy sense-objects"; according to Comy., this refers to some beings in the subhuman realms of existence, such as animals.

74. The PTS ed. omits this line and the next (*saṁsāraṁ nātivattare/etam ādīnavaṁ ñatvā*). The translation follows the Burmese-script text.

75. Though pleasurable, sensual pleasures are bound up with danger (*ādīnava*) in that they are impermanent and never fully satisfying. Thus they lead to frustration and to the perpetuation of the "round." The "danger" in them is to be seen as the noble truth of suffering.

76. The bond of sensual desire is what holds living beings to the sense-sphere realm (*kāmadhātu*), the bond of (desire for) being is what holds beings to saṁsāra. All those from the worldling through the once-returner (*sakadāgāmī*) are still bound by both bonds; the non-returner (*anāgāmī*) has eradicated the sensual bond but not the desire for being; the arahant has eradicated both bonds.

77. The Pātimokkha, the disciplinary rules of the Order of bhikkhus.

78. See Sutta 82 and note 45.

79. On the "All" see Sutta 7 and The Ones, note 5. The last line also appears in Suttas 66 and 68.

80. Comy. explains that the first verse refers to the giving of material things; the second—by the mentioning of "proclaiming" and "hearing"—refers to the gift of the Dhamma.

81. *Lapitalāpana*. The Buddha is referring derogatively to the brahmins' practice of reciting from the Vedic

scriptures. The threefold knowledge (*tevijja*) traditionally meant knowledge of the three Vedas, but the Buddha redefines this from the standpoint of the Dhamma as the knowledge leading to enlightenment and release from the round of births. The idea of persuasive talk or "patter" is a beggar's ploy to cajole people into giving alms.

The Section of The Fours

1. Accessible to entreaties (*yācayoga*), that is, always ready to teach the Dhamma when asked; and open-handed (*payatapāṇi*), being in constant readiness to give a gift, here the gift of the Dhamma, in the appropriate manner.

2. The Buddha is called "the great physician" as he offers the treatment to cure the suffering inherent in the round of births and deaths. And he is a surgeon (*sallakatta*) who has the method for excising the poisoned arrows (*salla*) of lust, hate and delusion embedded in the minds of beings.

3. This is the Buddha's variation on the brahmins' claim to be born from the mouth of the god Brahmā.

4. *Yāga*: a sacrificial offering or alms-giving.

5. The first three are included among the allowable ascetic practices (*dhutanga*). All four constitute the minimal requisites for living the bhikkhu life, taught as such in the ceremony of higher ordination (*upasampadā*).

6. See Sutta 62 and notes.

7. *Itibhavābhavahetu*: "by reason of being or not being thus." Explained by the Comy. as gain or loss, success or failure, increase or decrease.

8. *Brahmā* means the highest, best, foremost (of

beings) and a brahmā god exemplifies the state of one who maintains the practice of the *brahmavihāras*, the "divine abidings" of loving-kindness, compassion, sympathetic joy and equanimity. It is parents too who maintain these attitudes of love towards their children.

9. One's parents are like the earliest or first devas, divinities in the sense of being powerful guardians and protectors. They are also one's first teachers, teaching the most basic things, how to walk, talk, eat, etc., and about the people and objects in one's environment.

10. *Sugata.* Here meaning the disciples of the Buddha, according to the Comy., which glosses the word with *sammā paṭipanna.*

11. Arahants.

12. Those home-loving layfolk, attached to the household life, practise the worldly (*lokiya*) Dhamma of alms-giving, etc., which leads to heaven.

13. *Gaha*, literally "seizer," is also another name for the crocodile, although translated in Sutta 69 as "sharks," because of the ocean setting. *Rakkhasa* is, in Indian mythology, a kind of flesh-eating demon living in lakes and pools and in the ocean.

14. *Orambhāgiya-saṁyojana*: "the fetters belonging to the hither shore" or "lower fetters" are the first five fetters—personality view, doubt, clinging to external observances, sensual craving and ill will. They are called thus because they bind one to rebirth in the lower world, the sense-sphere realm. They are finally overcome at the stage of the non-returner.

15. *Sahāpi dukkhena jaheyya kāme.* Comy. explains this by reference to one who attains jhāna and the path with painful progress (*dukkhapaṭipadā*), i.e. who can

suppress the defilement of sensuality only with trouble and difficulty.

16. By "the world" is meant the noble truth of suffering, the world of experience consisting of form, feeling, perception, mental formations and consciousness. These are the five aggregates, equated with suffering in the exposition of the four noble truths.

17. He has finished with *kamma*, deeds which will produce a result in a future birth.

18. "Brahma-wheel" (*brahma-cakka*) is synonymous with Dhamma-wheel. The commencement of the Buddha's teaching career is referred to as "the setting in motion of the Dhamma-wheel," which is also the title of the famous sutta containing the first sermon proclaimed in the Deer Park at Benares.

KEY TO ABBREVIATIONS

BPS	Buddhist Publication Society
Comy.	Itivuttaka Commentary
Dhp.	Dhammapada
M.	Majjhima Nikāya
Netti	Nettippakaraṇa
PTS	Pali Text Society
S.	Saṁyutta Nikāya
Ud.	Udāna
Vism.	Visuddhimagga

BIBLIOGRAPHY

Editions of the Itivuttaka consulted:

Itivuttaka, edited by Ernst Windisch. Pali Text Society, reprinted 1975 (Roman script).

Khuddakanikāya, Vol. I, Chaṭṭhasangāyana edition of the Tipitaka, 1956 (Burmese script).

Khuddakanikāya, Part I, Ceylon Government, Buddha Jayanthi Tripitaka Series, Vol. 24, 1960 (Sinhala script).

Khuddakanikāya, Vol. I, Nālandā Devanāgarī Pāli Series, Bihar Government, 1959 (Devanāgarī script).

Editions of the Itivuttaka Commentary (*Paramatthadīpanī*) consulted:

Paramatthadīpanī of Dhammapālācariya, edited by M.M. Bose, 2 vols. PTS, reprinted 1977.

Other works consulted:

Bodhi, Bhikkhu. *The Discourse on the All-Embracing Net of Views*. BPS, 1978

Horner, I.B. *The Middle Length Sayings,* 3 volumes. PTS, 1954-59. (Translation of Majjhima Nikāya.)

Ireland, John D. *Saṁyutta Nikāya: An Anthology,* Part I, Wheel No. 107/109. BPS, 1967.

________. *The Udāna: Inspired Utterances of the Buddha.* BPS, 1990.

Ñāṇamoli, Bhikkhu. *The Guide*. PTS, 1962. (Translation of Nettippakaraṇa.)

________. *The Life of the Buddha.* BPS, 1972.

________. *The Path of Purification.* Colombo, 1956. (Translation of Visuddhimagga.)

Ñāṇananda, Bhikkhu. *Concept and Reality in Early Buddhist Thought.* BPS, 2nd ed., 1976.

Nyanaponika Thera. *Anguttara Nikāya, An Anthology,* Part I. Wheel No. 155/158. BPS, 1981.

Woodward, F.L. *The Minor Anthologies of the Pāli Canon,* Part II. PTS, reprinted 1948. (Translation of Udāna and Itivuttaka.)

________. *The Book of the Gradual Sayings,* Vols. I and II. PTS, 1932-33. (Translation of Anguttara Nikāya, Books 1 to 4.)

INDEX OF SUTTAS

THE SECTION OF THE TWOS (Dukanipāta)

THE SECTION OF THE THREES (*Tikanipāta*)

Available from BPS

THE UDĀNA

Inspired Utterances of the Buddha

Translated from the Pali by
John D. Ireland

The *Udāna* is one of the loveliest and most uplifting texts in the Pali Canon, a collection of eighty short but deeply impressive suttas. Opening at the foot of the Bodhi tree shortly after the Buddha's Enlightenment, the *Udāna* records some of the best known incidents in the Master's life: his paeon of victory over the forces of darkness; his instructions to Bāhiya on "sudden awakening"; the story of Nanda and the pink-footed nymphs; the parable of the blind men and the elephant; the solemn Nibbāna suttas; and much more. Like the *Dhammapada*, the *Udāna* will be a constant friend and advisor for frequent reading and reflection. It will also be a much appreciated gift to offer to friends receptive to the Dhamma. This new translation combines precision with clarity and also includes over 25 pages of notes drawn mostly from the Udāna Commentary.

THE BUDDHIST PUBLICATION SOCIETY

is an approved charity dedicated to making known the Teaching of the Buddha, which has a vital message for people of all creeds.

Founded in 1958, the BPS has published a wide variety of books and booklets covering a great range of topics. Its publications include accurate annotated translations of the Buddha's discourses, standard reference works, as well as original contemporary expositions of Buddhist thought and practice. These works present Buddhism as it truly is—a dynamic force which has influenced receptive minds for the past 2500 years and is still as relevant today as it was when it first arose.

A full list of our publications will be sent free of charge upon request. Write to:

The Hony. Secretary
BUDDHIST PUBLICATION SOCIETY
P.O. Box 61
54, Sangharaja Mawatha
Kandy Sri Lanka